If you like excitement, mystery and adventure you
will certainly like the castles and historic houses
of England, Wales, Scotland and Ireland.

Did you know that just over a hundred years ago
children were being executed for stealing and the
executions were public ones?

Did you know that Hampton Court Palace is said
to echo with the shriekings of Katherine Howard's
ghost?

Would you like to join the quest for King Arthur?

Other books by GYLES BRANDRETH

DOMINO GAMES AND PUZZLES
NUMBER GAMES AND PUZZLES
GAMES AND PUZZLES WITH COINS AND MATCHES
PENCIL AND PAPER GAMES AND PUZZLES
HOTCHPOTCH
THE ROYAL QUIZ BOOK
BRAIN-TEASERS AND MIND-BENDERS

All published by CORGI-CAROUSEL BOOKS

Project:
Castles and
Historic Houses

Gyles Brandreth

Illustrated by Rowan Barnes Murphy

**CAROUSEL BOOKS**
A DIVISION OF TRANSWORLD PUBLISHERS LTD

# PROJECT: CASTLES AND HISTORIC HOUSES

A CAROUSEL BOOK 0 552 54121 4

First publication in Great Britain

PRINTING HISTORY
Carousel edition published 1977

Carousel Books are published by
Transworld Publishers Ltd.,
Century House, 61-63, Uxbridge Road,
Ealing W5 5SA

Made and printed in Great Britain by the Guernsey Press Co. Ltd.,
Guernsey, Channel Islands.

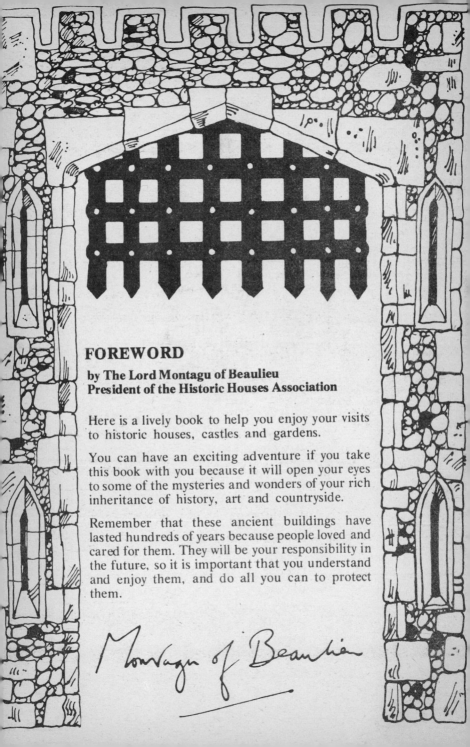

## FOREWORD

### by The Lord Montagu of Beaulieu
### President of the Historic Houses Association

Here is a lively book to help you enjoy your visits to historic houses, castles and gardens.

You can have an exciting adventure if you take this book with you because it will open your eyes to some of the mysteries and wonders of your rich inheritance of history, art and countryside.

Remember that these ancient buildings have lasted hundreds of years because people loved and cared for them. They will be your responsibility in the future, so it is important that you understand and enjoy them, and do all you can to protect them.

*Montagu of Beaulieu*

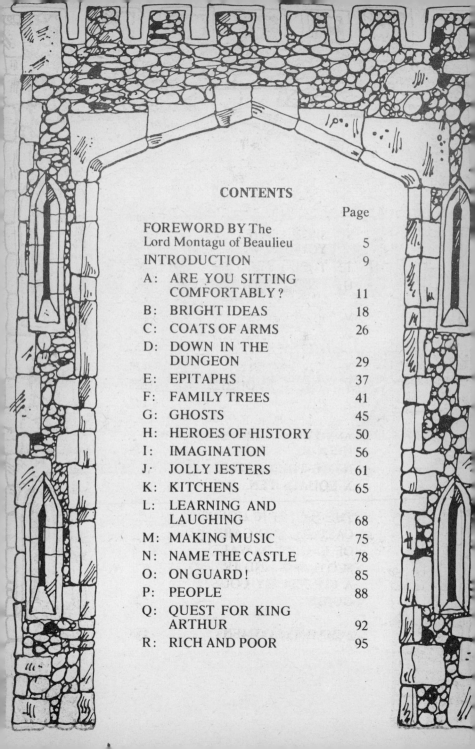

## CONTENTS

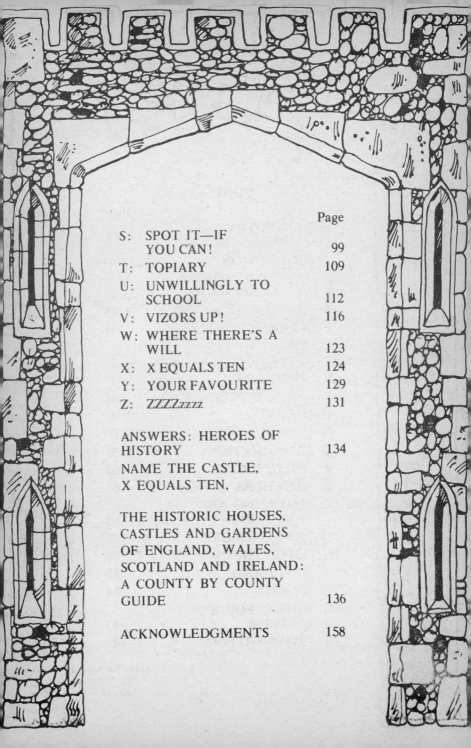

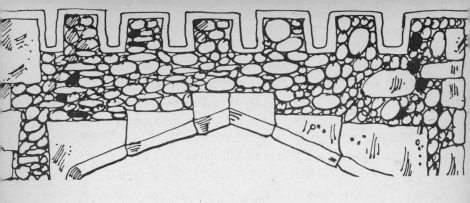

# INTRODUCTION

If you think you like excitement, adventure and mystery, you will certainly like the, castles and historic houses of England, Wales, Scotland and Ireland. They are extraordinary places, fascinating to learn about and wonderful to visit. When you go to one, you step into another world—not always better than the everyday world we know, not always worse, but almost always *different* and, often, very, very different indeed.

There are hundreds of historic buildings and gardens you can visit—and I've listed nearly all of them at the back of the book so you should be able to find a few near you!—and they range from mighty castles and gigantic stately homes to ancient ruins and tiny workmen's cottages. I have five favourites: Blenheim Palace in Oxfordshire, the home of the Duke of Marlborough and the birthplace of Sir Winston Churchill; Furzey Folk Cottage, near Lyndhurst in Hampshire, which was built in 1560 and where fourteen children once slept together in one small room; Churche's Mansion, a fine town house in Nantwich, Cheshire; the romantic

Dunrobin Castle in Sutherland in Scotland; and Blue Bridge House at Halstead in Essex, home of John Morley, 'England's most remarkable butcher'! By the time you have visited a few castles and historic houses, you too will have your favourites. When you get to page 129 you will see that you can even 'Vote for your favourite historic building'. Be sure you do.

This is a Project Book, which means it doesn't just tell you facts about castles and historic houses: it also gives you ideas of things to do, items to watch out for, points to remember, projects to pursue. I have tried to make it an entertaining A to Z that will help you explore and enjoy the old buildings you and I and all of us are lucky enough to be able to visit.

GYLES BRANDRETH

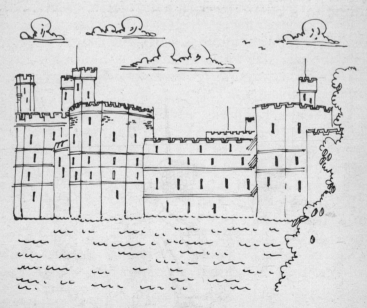

**Caernarfon Castle**

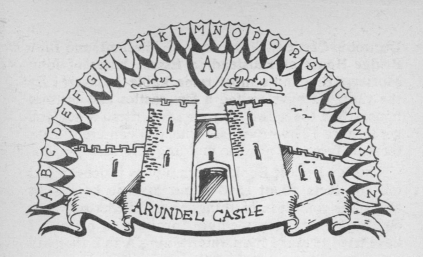

ARUNDEL CASTLE

## ARE YOU SITTING COMFORTABLY?

If you *are* sitting comfortably, then you are probably sitting in a chair that looks like this:

**Or this :**

**Or even this :**

The chairs you see in castles and historic houses don't look like the chairs you usually sit on at home. Here's one you could have seen when Queen Anne was Queen (1702-1714). Its frame is made of walnut:

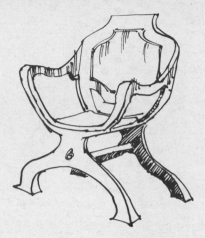

This chair is called a Chinese Chair and you could have seen it when Charles II was on the throne (1660-1685):

Here are two chairs you could have seen when James I was King (1603-1625).

This one is an armchair made of oak:

And this one is called a Farthingale chair:

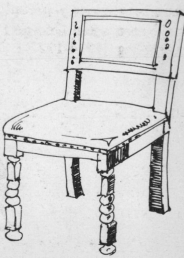

Here is a chair you could have seen when William and Mary were King (1689-1702) and Queen (1689-1694):

And here is one you could have seen when George I was King (1714-1727):

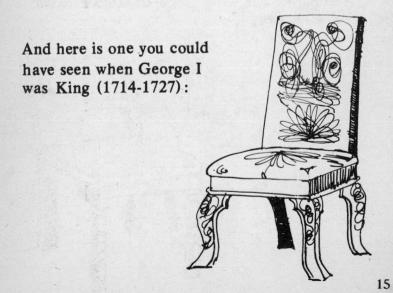

You could have seen this beautiful chair when George II was King (1727-1760):

This chair was made by a great and famous craftsman called George Hepplewhite. He died in 1786 when George III was King (1760-1820). The chair is made of mahogany:

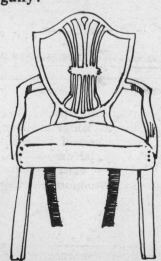

As it happens, you don't need to have been alive when Anne and Charles II and George III and James I and George II and William and Mary and George I were on the throne of England. You can see all eight of them today in one place: **Berkeley Castle** in Gloucestershire. There are fascinating chairs in every castle and historic house. When you look at them, try to imagine what the first person who ever sat in them must have looked like.

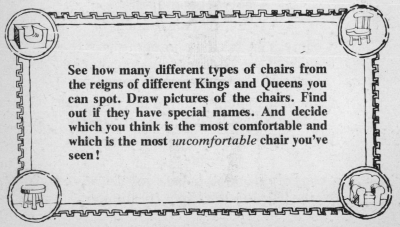

See how many different types of chairs from the reigns of different Kings and Queens you can spot. Draw pictures of the chairs. Find out if they have special names. And decide which you think is the most comfortable and which is the most *uncomfortable* chair you've seen!

BODIAM CASTLE

## BRIGHT IDEAS

The castles and historic houses of England, Wales, Scotland and Ireland are remarkable places, beautiful to look at, exciting to explore. When you visit one, go properly equipped. Here are some items to remember:

A notebook and pen

A sketchpad and pencil

A camera for taking photographs of the outside of the building (you may not be allowed to take pictures inside)

A compass to help you find out if you are going North, South, East or West

Your own list of things you want to look out for

A copy of this book in case you see any of the items in the 'Spot It' chapter

By the time you have been through this book from A to Z you should have a lot of bright ideas of what to do and what not to miss when you visit an historic building. To get you started, here is a list of fifty odds and ends to look out for and questions to ask yourself when you are visiting a castle or historic house.

1. **QUESTION:** What sort of everyday life did the man lead for whom this house was built?

2. **LOOK OUT FOR:** Animals' feet as the designs for the feet of chairs and tables.

3. **QUESTION:** Where did the children sleep in this house?

4. **LOOK OUT FOR:** Different forms of lighting and different kinds of lighting equipment, from candlesticks to chandeliers.

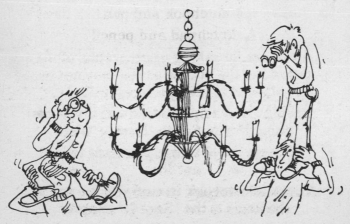

**5. QUESTION:** How many servants were needed to look after a house this size?

**6. LOOK OUT FOR:** Coats of Arms.

**7. QUESTION:** Where did the servants sleep?

**8. LOOK OUT FOR:** Teapots designed to look like something else—cottages or bee hives.

**9. QUESTION:** In which rooms did the lady of the house spend which part of her day?

**10. LOOK OUT FOR:** Chairs in paintings—and see how differently people used to sit in their chairs!

**11. QUESTION:** Why didn't people draw in their drawing rooms?

**12. LOOK OUT FOR:** Painted ceilings.

**13. QUESTION:** Where did the children play in the daytime?

14. **LOOK OUT FOR:** A teacup without handles.

15. **QUESTION:** At what time of day did the owners of the house usually get up?

16. **LOOK OUT FOR:** Dogs in paintings.

17. **QUESTION:** At what time of day did the servants of the house usually get up?

18. **LOOK OUT FOR:** Paintings in which the men are wearing wigs.

19. **QUESTION:** How was the room you are looking at once heated?

20. **LOOK OUT FOR:** A three-pronged fork.

21. **QUESTION:** At what time of day did people eat their main meal?

22. **LOOK OUT FOR:** Paintings in which the ladies are wearing crowns or tiaras.

**23. QUESTION:** Where did the children learn their lessons?

**24. LOOK OUT FOR:** Tapestries hanging on the walls.

**25. QUESTION:** How did the people call for their servants when the servants were in another room?

**26. LOOK OUT FOR:** Paintings of landscapes—find out where they are and how the scene has changed over the years.

**27. QUESTION:** What kind of food did the owners of the house eat?

**28. LOOK OUT FOR:** Chamberpots.

**29. QUESTION:** What kind of food did the servants eat?

**30. LOOK OUT FOR:** Paintings or carvings on ceilings that tell a story.

**31. QUESTION:** What did the owners of the houses *do* all day?

**32. LOOK OUT FOR:** Poems or pictures scratched onto the glass in windows.

**33. QUESTION:** How did the owners of the houses entertain themselves in the evenings?

**34. LOOK OUT FOR:** Very thick walls that may contain secret passages.

**35. QUESTION:** What time did the owners of the houses and their servants go to bed?

**36. LOOK OUT FOR:** Rooms completely panelled with wood.

**37. QUESTION:** In the past did the house ever have real lavatories?

**38. LOOK OUT FOR:** Windows that aren't windows at all—but have been painted on to the house to look like real windows.

**39. QUESTION:** How and how often did the owners of the houses wash?

**40. LOOK OUT FOR:** 'Library steps' for getting at the books on the top shelves.

**41. QUESTION:** How often did the owners of the houses go to church?

**42. LOOK OUT FOR:** Different styles of old shoes and footwear.

**43. QUESTION:** How old were the children when they left home?

**44. LOOK OUT FOR:** Warming pans.

**45. QUESTION:** Who was the most important person ever to have lived in or visited this house?

**46. LOOK OUT FOR:** Flags and banners.

**47. QUESTION:** Why are you being allowed to look around this house today when once upon a time the owners did not allow visitors to see their homes?

**48. LOOK OUT FOR:** Copper-plate handwriting and quill pens.

**49. QUESTION:** Would you like to live in the house you are visiting? If you would, why? If you wouldn't, why not?

**50. LOOK OUT FOR:** Musical instruments.

Whenever you see something you like and admire in a castle or an historic house—a rapier, an iron kettle, a painting of a dog, a beautiful dress, a card table, a dolls' house, a silver candlestick—make a note of it and draw a picture of it in your notebook. After a while, you will have collected enough items to furnish a stately home of your own.

ABCDEFGHIJKLMNOPQRSTUVWXYZ

COLCHESTER CASTLE

## COATS OF ARMS

When you visit a castle or an historic house you will almost certainly see the Coat of Arms of the family that lives or once lived there. A complete display of Arms—like the one opposite—is called an 'achievement' and here are the proper names given to its different parts:

1. **THE SHIELD.** This is the most important item as it carries the special design that represents the family and its name. The design is called a **CHARGE.** Many Coats of Arms consist only of a shield like this.

2. **THE HELMET.** The type of helmet shows the rank of the holder.

3. **THE MANTLING.** This swirling piece of drapery is useful when you are designing an achievement: you can use it to fill in any gaps in your design!

4. **THE WREATH or TORSE.** This was usually made of a twist of material.

26

5. **THE CREST.** Crests are decorative objects fixed to the top of helmets.

6. **THE SUPPORTERS.** It is usually royal or ducal Coats of Arms that have supporters and they can be animals or people.

7. **THE COMPARTMENT.** This is what the supporters stand on and it is usually either earth or water.

8. **THE MOTTO.** Not all achievements have a motto, but if they do it is usually written on a scroll and positioned in a prominent place.

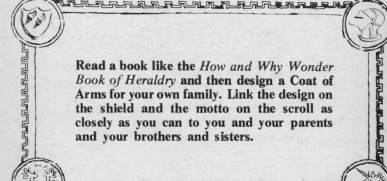

Read a book like the *How and Why Wonder Book of Heraldry* and then design a Coat of Arms for your own family. Link the design on the shield and the motto on the scroll as closely as you can to you and your parents and your brothers and sisters.

DUNROBIN CASTLE

## DOWN IN THE DUNGEON

Torture has never been lawful in the United Kingdom. All the same, in the past—and as recently as two hundred years ago—people kept as prisoners in the dungeons of great castles *were* tortured. The instruments of torture were truly terrible.

Iron collars were placed around the prisoners' necks and slowly tightened:

Stretched on the rack a man could have nine inches added to the length of his body:

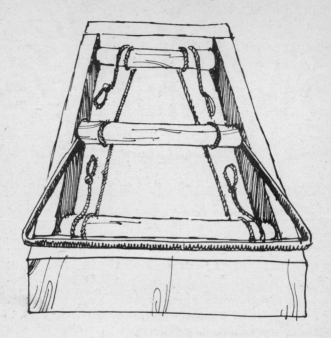

Pincers were used for extracting or breaking prisoners' teeth:

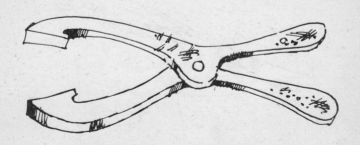

Thumbscrews were used for breaking their fingers and thumbs:

Tweezers were used for tearing off their finger-nails:

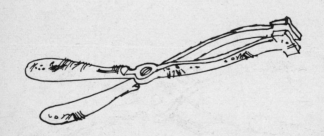

During the reign of Henry VIII (1509-1547) the Constable of the Tower of London was a particularly cruel man called Skeffington. He invented a hideous instrument of torture which was used in the dungeons of the Tower. It was an iron frame which closed round the prisoner. It was nicknamed 'Skeffington's Daughter':

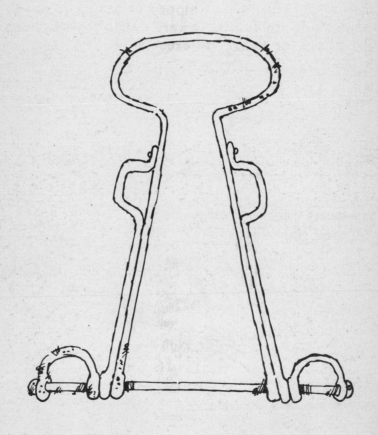

Kings and Queens and powerful lords usually only tortured their prisoners if they wanted to get information out of them or force them to confess to crimes they had (or had not) committed. Ordinary criminals were not usually imprisoned for long periods. The idea of punishing people by putting them in prison for sentences lasting several years is not much more than a hundred years old. In the more distant past, criminals were given a physical punishment (they were whipped or beaten or put to the ducking stool) or they were put in the stocks or the pillory, or they were executed.

The ducking stool.

# The stocks.

# The scaffold.

The gallows.

Only just over a hundred years ago children were being executed for stealing and the executions were public ones. The biggest crowd ever to watch an execution in England was in 1641 when over 200,000 came to Tower Green to see Thomas, Earl of Strafford, Lord Lieutenant of Ireland, being beheaded. Fortunately, the death penalty was abolished in the United Kingdom in 1965.

Find out the name of all the Kings and Queens of England who have ever been imprisoned in a dungeon or executed in public. Find out where they were kept prisoner and who ordered their executions.

EDINBURGH CASTLE

# EPITAPHS

In the towns and villages near the castles and historic houses you visit you will always find a church, and by the church you will almost always find a churchyard. In the churchyard will be gravestones and on the gravestones will be epitaphs—lines and verses about the people buried there. They can be fascinating to read. Here is one from a tomb at Bath Abbey:

*Here lies Ann Mann;*
*She lived an old Maid and*
*She died an old Mann.*

**And here is one from the grave of a Shropshire blacksmith:**

*My sledge and anvil lie declined,*
*My bellows too have lost their wind;*
*My fire's extinct, my forge decay'd,*
*And in the dust my body's laid:*
*My coal is out, my iron's gone,*
*My nails are drove, my work is done.*

**Here is one from a churchyard in Sevenoaks, Kent:**

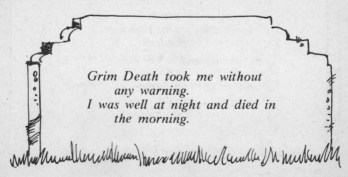

*Grim Death took me without*
*any warning.*
*I was well at night and died in*
*the morning.*

Here, from Gateshead churchyard, Durham, is the epitaph of Robert Trollop, a local architect and builder:

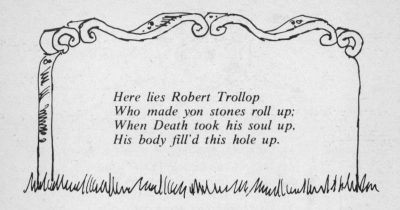

Here lies Robert Trollop
Who made yon stones roll up;
When Death took his soul up,
His body fill'd this hole up.

In Hyden churchyard in Yorkshire you can read this unusual epitaph:

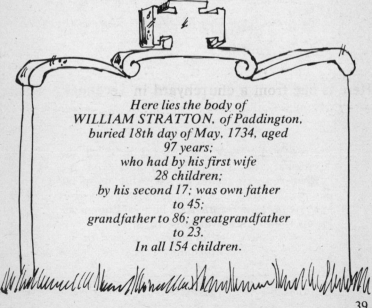

Here lies the body of
WILLIAM STRATTON, of Paddington,
buried 18th day of May, 1734, aged
97 years;
who had by his first wife
28 children;
by his second 17; was own father
to 45;
grandfather to 86; greatgrandfather
to 23.
In all 154 children.

And here is a much simpler epitaph. You will find it on the grave of Richard Groombridge in Horsham, Sussex:

He was.

Keep a notebook and record in it all the unusual and interesting epitaphs you see when you visit a churchyard. And if you see any interesting messages or mottos carved in stone or wood on parts of houses and castles you visit, make a note of them too.

FARNHAM CASTLE

# FAMILY TREES

In many of the guide books of the castles and historic houses you visit you will find family trees. This is the family tree of the Watsons who live at **Rockingham Castle** in Northamptonshire. It starts with Edward Watson, who lived at Rockingham Castle when Henry VIII was King, and traces the family through thirteen generations to James, Fiona and David Watson, who were born in 1961, 1965 and 1968, and who live in the Castle today:

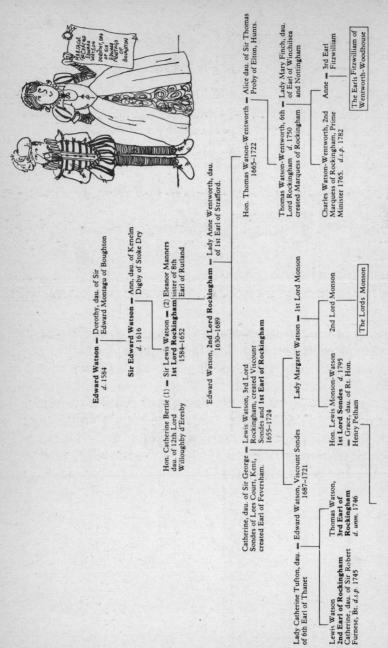

Edward Watson = Dorothy, dau. of Sir
d. 1584    Edward Montagu of Boughton

Sir Edward Watson = Ann, dau. of Kenelm
d. 1616    Digby of Stoke Dry

Hon. Catherine Bertie (1) = Sir Lewis Watson = (2) Eleanor Manners
dau. of 12th Lord    1st Lord Rockingham    sister of 8th
Willoughby d'Eresby    1584–1652    Earl of Rutland

Edward Watson, 2nd Lord Rockingham = Lady Anne Wentworth, dau.
1630–1689    of 1st Earl of Strafford.

Catherine, dau. of Sir George = Lewis Watson, 3rd Lord
Sondes of Lees Court, Kent,    Rockingham, created Viscount
created Earl of Feversham.    Sondes and 1st Earl of Rockingham
    1655–1724

Hon. Thomas Watson-Wentworth = Alice dau. of Sir Thomas
1665–1722    Proby of Elton, Hunts.

Thomas Watson-Wentworth, 6th = Lady Mary Finch, dau.
Lord Rockingham    d. 1750    of Earl of Winchilsea
created Marquess of Rockingham    and Nottingham

Charles Watson-Wentworth, 2nd    Anne = 3rd Earl
Marquess of Rockingham, Prime    Fitzwilliam
Minister 1765.    d.s.p. 1782

The Earls Fitzwilliam of
Wentworth-Woodhouse

Lady Catherine Tufton, dau. = Edward Watson, Viscount Sondes    Lady Margaret Watson = 1st Lord Monson
of 6th Earl of Thanet    1687–1721

    2nd Lord Monson

Lewis Watson,    Thomas Watson,    Hon. Lewis Monson-Watson
2nd Earl of Rockingham    3rd Earl of    1st Lord Sondes d. 1795
Catherine, dau. of Sir Robert    Rockingham    = Grace, dau. of Rt. Hon.
Furnese, Bt. d.s.p. 1745    d. unm. 1746    Henry Pelham

The Lords Monson

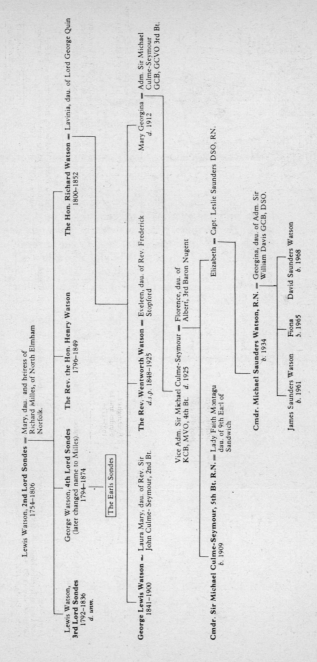

Lewis Watson, 2nd Lord Sondes = Mary, dau. and heiress of
1754–1806     Richard Milles, of North Elmham
           Norfolk.

Lewis Watson,
3rd Lord Sondes
1792–1836
d. unm.

George Watson, 4th Lord Sondes
(later changed name to Milles)
1794–1874

The Earls Sondes

The Rev. the Hon. Henry Watson
1796–1849

The Hon. Richard Watson = Lavinia, dau. of Lord George Quin
1800–1852

George Lewis Watson = Laura Mary, dau. of Rev. Sir
1841–1900     John Culme-Seymour, 2nd Bt.

The Rev. Wentworth Watson = Eveleen, dau. of Rev. Frederick
d.s.p. 1848–1925     Stopford

Mary Georgina = Adm. Sir Michael
d. 1912      Culme-Seymour
         GCB, GCVO 3rd Bt.

Vice Adm. Sir Michael Culme-Seymour = Florence, dau. of
KCB, MVO, 4th Bt.    d. 1925     Albert, 3rd Baron Nugent

Cmdr. Sir Michael Culme-Seymour, 5th Bt. R.N. = Lady Faith Montagu
b. 1909     dau. of 9th Earl of
       Sandwich

Elizabeth = Capt. Leslie Saunders DSO, R.N.

Cmdr. Michael Saunders Watson, R.N. = Georgina, dau. of Adm. Sir
b. 1934     William Davis GCB, DSO.

James Saunders Watson
b. 1961

Fiona
b. 1965

David Saunders Watson
b. 1968

**PROJECT!**

Draw up your own family tree and see how far back in history you can trace your own family. Get your parents and grandparents and uncles and aunts to help you and learn all about family trees by reading a book like *A Monster at the Top of the Tree* by Kathleen Menhinick Dewey.

GLAMIS CASTLE

# GHOSTS

There are very few castles and historic houses that *don't* have a ghost or two! The guide books may not tell you about them because they don't want to frighten you, but if you are someone who isn't frightened by creaking floorboards and mysterious happenings make sure you *ask* as soon as you get to the castle or house you are going to visit whether or not it's haunted. You are very unlikely to see or hear a ghost yourself, but you can at least have a look at the spot where the ghastly ghosties are supposed to appear.

On the following pages are some of the famous and not-so-famous places that people believe could be haunted—

**Windsor Castle** is said to have several royal ghosts, including Elizabeth I, Charles I and George III.

Katherine Howard, the fourth of Henry VIII's six wives, was beheaded in 1542. The Haunted Gallery at **Hampton Court Palace** is said to echo still to the shriekings of her ghost.

There is a marvellous moat around **Scotney Castle** at Lamberhurst in Kent. Now and again the villagers have seen the ghost of a drowned tax collector crawling out of the moat in the dead of night.

The ghost of Bonnie Prince Charlie haunts **Culloden House,** east of Inverness in Scotland, and nearby the site of the famous Battle of Culloden Moor in 1746 is haunted by many ghosts—including an army in the sky.

**Castle Coch,** just north of Cardiff in Wales, is haunted by the ghost of a man who secretly buried treasure in hidden underground passages beneath the castle's foundations. People claim to have seen the ghost. No one has seen the treasure!

The ghost of Lady Lisgar haunts **Bosworth Hall** in Leicestershire. She was condemned to haunt the place after her death because she once refused to let a priest into the house to attend a maidservant who was dying.

Find an old white sheet and turn it into a ghost costume. Cut out holes for the eyes so you can see where you are going and then do your best to haunt your family and friends. Terrify them with frightening screams and ghostly cackling!

## HISTORY'S HEROES

Here are some of the heroes and heroines of British history and the houses with which they have been associated—and which you can still visit to this day. If we tell you the names of all the places, can you put a name to all the faces?

1. Henry VIII's second wife lived here at **Hever Castle,** near Edenbridge in Kent. What was her name?

**2.** This is **Ann Hathaway's cottage** at Stratford-upon-Avon in Warwickshire.

Her husband was a poet and playwright. What was his name?

**3. Apsley House** was the London home of this great Duke, after whom the gumboot has been named.

What was his name?

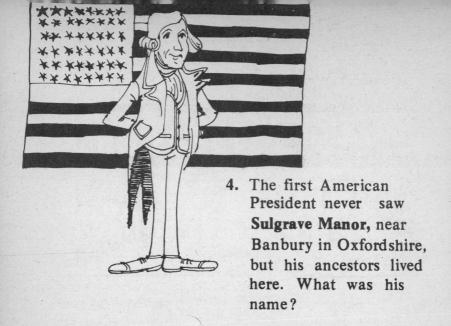

**4.** The first American President never saw **Sulgrave Manor,** near Banbury in Oxfordshire, but his ancestors lived here. What was his name?

**5.** This is **Sherborne Castle** in Dorset. The man who had the core of the castle built for him in 1594 also introduced tobacco and potatoes to the British Isles. What was his name?

6. 'The Lady with the Lamp' often visited **Claydon House** in Buckinghamshire after her sister married the owner in 1858. What was the lady's name?

7. One of Britain's greatest Prime Ministers lived at **Chartwell,** at Westerham in Kent. What was his name?

8. **Hill Top,** near Swarey in Cumbria, is a seventeenth century cottage where the lady who created Peter Rabbit, Benjamin Bunny, Mrs. Tiggy Winkle and many other delightful characters, once lived. What was her name?

9. **Hugheden Manor** at High Wycombe in Buckingham-shire was for thirty-five years the home of another of Britain's greatest Prime Ministers. He lived from 1804 to 1881 and was a good friend of Queen Victoria.

What was his name?

**10.** William Shakespeare wrote a famous play about a Scottish lord who became king himself by murdering King Duncan at **Cawdor Castle**, in Nairn in Scotland. What was his name?

Pick your own hero from history. Find out all you can about him or her—where he was born, where he lived, where he died, what he did, who his children were, whether his descendants are alive still. Collect all the information you can and keep it in a Hero's Scrapbook.

## IMAGINATION

When you visit a castle or an historic house don't leave your imagination with your coat in the car or the coach — take it with you. As you go into a great old building just imagine what life there must have been *really* like years and years ago. Imagine what the people who once lived there *really* did all day. Imagine how they dressed, imagine what they ate, imagine what they talked about and did to entertain themselves long before television was invented. Picture them — all of them: the grand lords and ladies *and* the hardworked servants who looked after them — and as you walk about the building *really* try to imagine you are walking in their shoes.

And if you feel like letting your imagination 'run riot', when you get back home you can put some of the things you have imagined down on paper. You can write poems and plays and stories about the figures from history you have learnt about. You can draw and paint pictures of the houses and gardens you have seen.

As well as imagining the past as it must really have been, you can also try imagining the past as you know it wasn't but it *might* have been! For example, if you go to a house like **Castle Howard** in Yorkshire and visit the Costume Gallery, don't just picture yourself in the beautiful clothes: imagine how you would have made clothes if you had been a designer two hundred years ago. How would you have dressed a lord and a lady in the reign of George III (1760-1820)?

When you visit a beautiful garden, like the **Great Comp Garden** near Borough Green in Kent, don't simply admire it. Imagine how you would have laid it out had you been a landscape gardener.

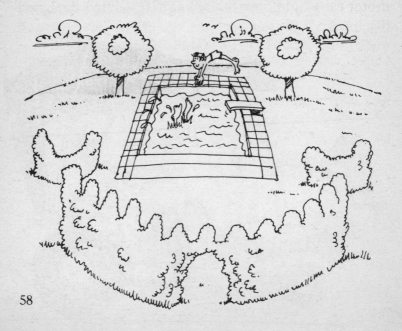

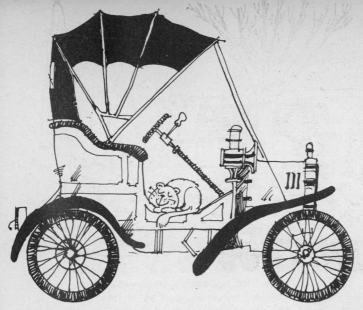

And when you visit somewhere like **Beaulieu** and look at all the cars in the National Motor Museum, don't simply imagine what it would be like to drive one of them: try to imagine what the first motor car would have looked like if *you* had designed it.

# PROJECT!

Imagine who you would most like to have been in the whole history of the world if you couldn't be yourself. You can choose to be anyone you like—Admiral Nelson, Elizabeth I, Guy Fawkes, Henry VIII's public executioner, the first Duke of Marlborough, the Duke of Marlborough's cook—but once you have chosen who you want to be find out all you can about them, and then see if you wouldn't rather be who you actually are!

JANE AUSTEN'S HOUSE

## JOLLY JESTERS

Many of the Kings and Queens of England have had
Court Jesters: men whose job it was to make the
monarch laugh. Even Queen Victoria had en-
tertainers come to court to amuse her: she found
midgets and dwarfs especially entertaining. When
Dan Leno, the great music hall star, went to entertain Edward VII at **Sandringham** at the beginning
of the century he was afterwards known as 'the
King's jester'. Henry VIII and most of the kings
before him had full-time jesters who lived at court:
they were known as 'fools' and sang and danced and
told jokes — often very cheeky jokes that no one else
at court would have dared to tell.

63

**PROJECT!**

Collect all the jokes you can think of and all the jokes you are told and write them down in a notebook. Call it your Court Jester's Joke Book. When you next get invited to Buckingham Palace or Windsor Castle, it could come in handy.

KENILWORTH CASTLE

## KITCHENS

The kitchens of yesterday were very different from the kitchens of today. There are so many things that we take for granted in a modern kitchen — the oven, the electric kettle, the tin and the tin opener, the refrigerator, the toaster, hot and cold running water — that simply did not exist a hundred years ago, which is why the kitchens you will see in castles and historic houses look so different from the everyday kitchens you know, and why so many people were needed to do all the work in the old kitchens.

# A KITCHEN IN THE LATE MIDDLE AGES

See the scullion boy turning
the spit on which the meat is
being roasted by the fire.

## A TUDOR KITCHEN

See the dog in the wheel
turning the spit on which the
meat is being roasted.

A VICTORIAN KITCHEN

PROJECT!

In his famous diary Samuel Pepys (1633-1703) wrote about a 'pretty dinner' he once had. It consisted of: 'a brace of stewed carp, six roasted chickens, a jowle of salmon, a tanzy (a dish of eggs and cream), two neat's tongues (ox-tongues) and cheese'. Write out the menu of the 'pretty dinner' you think you would most like to eat.

LANCASTER CASTLE

# LEARNING AND LAUGHING

Do you know the names of all the Kings and Queens of England from 1066 to the present day? You don't? Well, you should! And if you did, you would find visiting castles and historic houses that bit more interesting—especially if the castle or house happened to be one where royalty had once lived or stayed.

A hundred years ago every child had to learn the names and dates of all the English monarchs off by heart. School teachers were much stricter then and any child who didn't learn his lesson properly would be made to stand in the corner of the classroom wearing a dunce's cap *or* be made to write out the lesson over and over again *or* be rapped over the knuckles with a wooden ruler *or* (worst of all) be beaten on the bottom with a cane!

*You* won't be given the cane if you don't know the names of the Kings and Queens of England, but if you would like to learn them you will find them all listed with their dates in another special Carousel

68

paperback called *The Royal Quiz Book*. And if you enjoy learning poems off by heart, here is a verse that will remind you of all the monarchs' names from 1066 to 1901 :

Willie, Willie, Harry, Stee,
Harry, Dick, John, Harry Three,
One, Two, Three Neds, Richard Two,
Harry Four, Five, Six. Then who?
Edward Four, Five, Dick the Bad,
Harrys twain and Ned the lad,
Mary, Bessie, James the Vain,
Charlie, Charlie, James again,
William and Mary, Anna Gloria,
Four Georges, William and Victoria.

Once you have worked out that 'Stee' stands for Stephen, 'Ned' for Edward and 'Bessie' for Elizabeth, the verse should begin to make sense. Because it was written when Victoria was Queen it doesn't go beyond her reign. Here are four more lines to bring it up to 1952, the year in which George VI died and Elizabeth II came to the throne.


Edward Seventh next, and then
George the Fifth in 1910.
Edward the Eighth soon abdicated
And so a George was reinstated.


Discipline at home was nearly as strict as discipline at school. The Victorians had a saying that children 'should be seen and not heard'! The children of richer families spent most of their time in the nursery being looked after by a nanny or a governess. Poorer children spent more time with their parents, but they were still expected to behave themselves properly, playing quietly together and not speaking until they were spoken to.

Many of the games played by Victorian children are games children still play today—Snakes and Ladders, Ludo, Beggar My Neighbour, Draughts, Dominoes, Charades, Blind Man's Buff, Sardines and all—but nowadays a child who loses a game doesn't have to do what the Victorian child did and 'pay a forfeit'. A hundred years ago whoever lost a game had to pay a 'forfeit'. It was a sort of punishment for losing, but it wasn't a *real* punishment at all. Most of the 'forfeits' were fun ones, as you can find out for yourself now. These thirty 'forfeits' come

70

from a Victorian book of games. When you next play a game at home, make sure the loser pays a proper 'forfeit'.

### FORFEITS

1. Bow to the wittiest, kneel to the prettiest, and kiss the one you love best.

2. Bite an inch off the poker.—This is done by holding the poker an inch from your mouth and then pretending to bite.

3. Lie down your full length upon the floor, fold your arms and rise without unfolding them.

4. Push your friend's head through a ring.—This is done by putting your finger through a ring, and then pushing your friend's head with the tip of your finger.

5. Animal forfeit.—The forfeit payer must go to each of the company in turn and ask for the name of his favourite animal, and must then imitate the cry of that animal.

6. To dot and carry one.—Hold one ankle in one hand and hop round the room.

7. The deaf man.—The forfeit payer stands in the middle of the room and the company invite him to do certain things. To the first three invitations he must reply: "I am deaf, and cannot hear," but to the fourth invitation he must reply: 'I am no longer deaf,' and he is then bound to perform whatever the company suggest, no matter how disagreeable the task may be.

8. Put yourself through the keyhole.—Write the word "yourself" on a piece of paper and pass it through the keyhole.

9. Sit upon the fire.—Write "the fire" upon a piece of paper and then sit upon the paper.

10. Place a straw on the floor so that you cannot jump over it.—To do this you must place the straw close to the wall.

11. Laugh in one corner, cry in another, sing in a third, and dance in a fourth.

12. Put one hand where the other cannot touch it.—To do this you must clasp the left elbow with the right hand.

13. Say: "Quizzical quiz, kiss me quick," six times without taking breath.

14. Kiss a book inside and out without opening it.—This is done by kissing the book inside the room and outside the room.

15. Put two chairs back to back, then take off your shoes and jump over them.—This is a catch: it is the shoes you jump over, not the chairs.

16. Put a candle where everyone in the room, except yourself, can see it.—To do this you place it on your own head.

17. Repeat the letters of the alphabet three times, leaving out the letter "o" each time.

18. Take one of your friends upstairs and bring him down upon a feather.—Take someone upstairs, give him a feather and he will find down upon it, so you will have obeyed the command, "to bring him down upon a feather."

19. Repeat six times: 'Around the rugged rocks three ragged rascals ran a rural race.'

20. Repeat a piece of poetry, counting the words aloud. Thus: "Twinkle (one), twinkle (two), little (three) star (four), How (five) I (six) wonder (seven) what (eight) you (nine) are (ten)" and so on.

21. Become a statue.—You must stand on a chair and allow one of the company to place you in any ridiculous attitude he can think of.

22. Answer "It was I" to everything said to you.—Each person in the room may speak to you if he chooses. Suppose the first person says: "I saw a monkey today," the forfeit payer must reply: "It was I" and so on.

23. Comparisons.—The forfeit payer must compare someone in the room to some object, and then explain in which way he or she resembles or differs from it. For instance, a gentleman may compare a lady to a rose, because they are both sweet, though, unlike the rose, she is without a thorn.

24. Blow out a lighted candle blindfolded.— This is a much more difficult feat to perform than you would imagine; you are almost sure not to blow in the right direction.

25. Leave the room with two legs and return with six.—To do this you must bring a chair in with you.

26. Stand on a chair and make whatever grimaces you are bidden without smiling.

27. Stand on a chair and spell "opportunity."—This is an opportunity for the other children to kiss you or tease you in any way.

28. Repeat six times without a mistake: "A lump of rough light red leather, a red light rough leather lump."

29. Repeat six times: "There was an old woman who was a thistle sifter, she had a sieve full of sifted thistles, and a sieve full of unsifted thistles, and she was a thistle sifter."

30. Ask a question to which it is impossible to answer "no".—The question is "What does 'yes' spell?"

Find out all you can about what life was like for children a hundred or more years ago. What did their bedrooms look like at home? What did they learn at school? What were their clothes like? What were their toys like? Draw up a list of the ten best things and the ten worst things about being a child before the twentieth century.

# MAKING MUSIC

Many castles and historic houses have Music Rooms, where the owners once made music for themselves or paid professional musicians to come and play for them. They are rooms in which all three pieces of music on the next page might once have been played. The first is by Thomas Arne (1710-1778) who also wrote the music for *Rule, Britannia!* The second is by another English composer, Henry Purcell (1658-1695), who was royal composer to Charles II. The third piece is by the great German composer Johann Sebastian Bach (1685-1750).

The music is very simple and can be played on almost any instrument, but as it has been written out it is probably best suited to the piano or the recorder. If you are going to visit a famous house with a school party and the house has a Music Room, you could suggest to your teacher that he writes in advance to

## Minuet.

## Air.

## Minuet in G Minor.

the house you are going to visit to ask if you and your friends can bring your recorders and actually play one of the pieces of music in the Music Room.

When you visit a great house or castle be sure to find out when it was built. If you like music, remember the date when the house was built and see if you can find a record of a piece of music that was written round about the time the house was built. Many public libraries now lend records as well as books and they will be able to help you. You will be fascinated to hear the way in which music has changed across the centuries.

NEIDPATH CASTLE

# NAME THE CASTLE

Here are drawings of some of the most famous castles
in England, Wales, Scotland and Ireland. Can you
name them? To help you, the first and last letter of
each castle's name is given, and so is the county in
which you will find it. And once you have worked out
which castle is which, try to work out a way of visiting
some of them.

## 1. B - - - R CASTLE, PERTHSHIRE, SCOTLAND

## 2. W - - - - - R CASTLE, BERKSHIRE, ENGLAND

## 3. B - - - - - Y CASTLE, COUNTY CLARE, IRELAND

## 4. D - - R CASTLE, KENT, ENGLAND

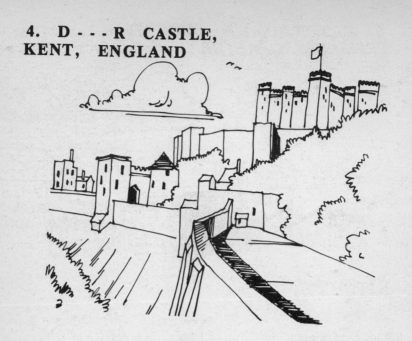

## 5. C - - K CASTLE, CLWYD, WALES

## 6.   CASTLE C - - - E,   COUNTY FERMANAGH, ULSTER

## 7.   B - - - - M CASTLE, SUSSEX, ENGLAND

## 8. W · · · · · K CASTLE, WARWICKSHIRE, ENGLAND

## 9. I · · · · · · · Y CASTLE, ARGYLL, SCOTLAND

# 10. S - - T M - - - - L'S M - - - T, CORNWALL, ENGLAND

Draw a map of the United Kingdom and Ireland and mark all the castles you can find on the map. You will be able to get a complete list of all the castles in England, Wales, Scotland and Ireland from any good library — and you will be amazed by how many there are. Any that you have visited, mark on the map in a special colour.

## ON GUARD!

A number of castles and historic houses have collections of toy soldiers and you will find a fairly long list of them in a very enjoyable book called *Discovering Toys and Toy Museums* by Pauline Flick.

Model soldiers have been in existence from ancient times, although the earliest examples may not have been intended as toys as we know them today. In fact throughout history there have been many famous collectors of model soldiers—among them several European kings and other men including Sir Winston Churchill, who was reputed to have 1500 models in his collection.

War games were introduced into England in Norman times and have been played by boys and girls of all ages ever since. In this space of time the models have varied from knights, both at war and in the field of tournaments, through the Civil War and the

Napoleonic Wars to the present day, and so the style of dress and weaponry has changed greatly.

The making of model soldiers has been carried on in many places from early times, with the materials used varying from clay to metal, those for the rich collectors being made from precious metals. In areas where wood-carving was most important the models were hand-carved and these were very popular in England where they were imported. In the 18th century Germany was one of the chief makers of tin soldiers which appeared as small flat models. It was not until 1868 that an Englishman, William Britain, began to make a hollow, moulded metal soldier, which completely overshadowed the German models and became the basis for a whole new field of model-making. Many of the original firms that copied the idea are still in business, including the originator, William Britain.

The toy that is reproduced on the opposite page is taken from a set of paper soldiers called 'The Castle of the Commander-in-Chief', which was made in Germany in 1840.

To make the figures stand, trace them on to thin card, cut out each figure and stick it on to a piece of card such as a postcard. Then support the figure by sticking a small piece of wood or plasticine behind the curved section at the foot of the model. They can then be arranged ready for action. Give them white trousers, with blue coats and red and gold trimmings. You may also like to try to devise a castle like the original one, which is made of wood blocks with the pictures pasted on them.

Choose one of the great battles of history and find out all you can about it. Learn the names of the generals and try to understand their tactics — why they fought the battle in the way they did. If you have toy soldiers of your own — or can make enough ones with card — you can even even try to recreate the battles of the past today.

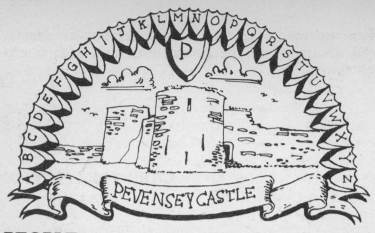

PEVENSEY CASTLE

# PEOPLE

You wouldn't be able to visit any castles or historic houses if it weren't for people—and not only the people who run the buildings now and the people who lived and worked in them in the past, but principally the people who designed and built the great houses, and all the beautiful furniture and furnishings you see inside them.

Here are four of Britain's most famous architects who flourished in the seventeenth and eighteenth centuries.

CHRISTOPHER WREN
(1632-1723)

INIGO JONES (1573-1652)

ROBERT ADAM
(1728-1792)

JOHN NASH
(1752-1835)

These architects' names are worth remembering, not only because they designed and built some of the country's most beautiful and important buildings, but also because their work influenced others and, visiting historic houses, you will often hear their names mentioned.

Here are three other men whose names you will often hear mentioned and whose work has helped make Britain's historic houses the beautiful places they are.

**GRINLING GIBBONS**
**(1648-1720)**
**Wood-carver and sculptor**

**LANCELOT**
**'CAPABILITY' BROWN**
**(1715-1783)**
**Landscape gardener**

# THOMAS CHIPPENDALE
## (1718-1779)
### Furniture designer

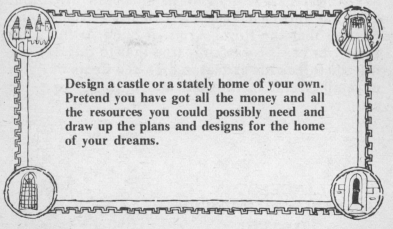

Design a castle or a stately home of your own.
Pretend you have got all the money and all
the resources you could possibly need and
draw up the plans and designs for the home
of your dreams.

# QUEST FOR KING ARTHUR

You have heard of King Arthur and his famous Knights of the Round Table. Historians now say he is a mythical character who never really lived, but medieval chroniclers believed in his existence and claimed that the Royal Arms of King Arthur were three crowns. It is certainly true that to this day you will see three crowns featured on the Coats of Arms of families and institutions and cities all over the country.

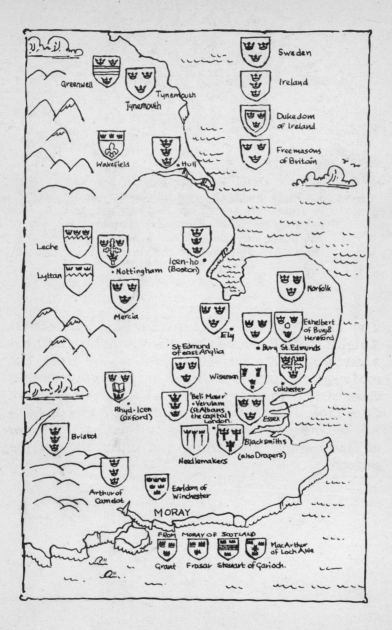

Greenwell

Tynemouth

Tynemouth

Wakefield

Hull

Sweden

Ireland

Dukedom of Ireland

Freemasons of Britain

Leche

Lyttan

Nottingham

Icen-ho (Boston)

Norfolk

Ely

Ethelbert of Bury & Hereford

Mercia

St Edmund of east Anglia

Bury St Edmunds

Wiseman

Colchester

Rhyd-Icen (Oxford)

'Beli Mawr' Verulam (St Albans the capital London)

Essex

Bristol

Needlemakers

Blacksmiths (also Drapers)

Arthur of Camelot

Earldom of Winchester

MORAY

FROM MORAY OF SCOTLAND

Grant    Frasar    Stewart of Garioch.

MacArthur of Loch Awe

# PROJECT!

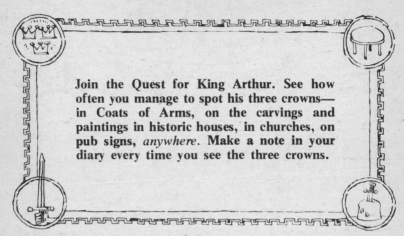

Join the Quest for King Arthur. See how often you manage to spot his three crowns— in Coats of Arms, on the carvings and paintings in historic houses, in churches, on pub signs, *anywhere*. Make a note in your diary every time you see the three crowns.

## RICH AND POOR

Remember that in the years before the twentieth century, for every rich Englishman there were several hundred poor ones! The princes and nobles may have led luxurious lives in their castles and mansions, but they all had lots of servants to look after them, and the servants worked incredibly long hours for very small wages.

To give you an idea of how many people could look after one member of the nobility, here is an extreme example: the household of Katherine Parr, sixth of Henry VIII's wives and the one who survived him.

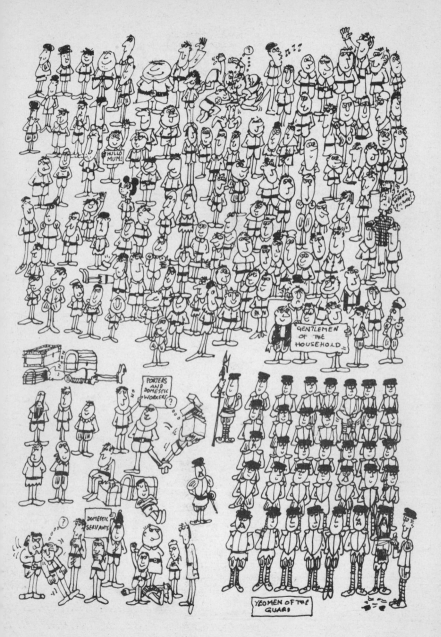

**PROJECT!**

If you had lived in the past and had worked as a servant in one of the great castles or historic houses of England, what kind of servant would you have wanted to be? A cook? A stable lad? A serving girl? A porter? A scullery maid? When you have decided on your job, find out all you can about it, and then choose the castle or house in which you think you would most like—or maybe *least dislike*—to have worked.

SKIPTON CASTLE

# SPOT IT — IF YOU CAN!

Here are items of every shape and size that you might easily find in one (or in more than one) of Britain's castles and historic houses. Look out for them and each time you spot one tick it off the list.

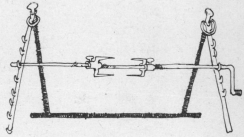

## 1. A LADY'S FAN

## 2. A ROASTING SPIT

**3. A PORTRAIT OR A PHOTOGRAPH OF QUEEN VICTORIA**

**4. A LATTICE WINDOW**

**5. A BISHOP'S MITRE**

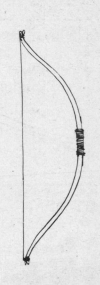

**6. A LONGBOW**

## 7. ARMOUR FOR A HORSE

## 8. AN ELIZABETHAN TABLE

## 9. A CLAY PIPE

## 11. A CHANDELIER

## 10. A CEILING PAINTING

## 12. A BELLROPE
## FOR CALLING
## THE SERVANTS

## 14. A PORTRAIT OF
## HENRY VIII

## 13. A SPINNING
## WHEEL

## 15. A LION AND A
## UNICORN

## 16. A TOWN CRIER'S BELL

## 17. A GENTLEMAN'S WIG

## 18. AN EIGHTEENTH CENTURY POST-CHAISE

## 19. A MUFF

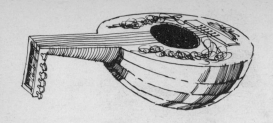

**20. A LUTE**

**21. A SWORD**

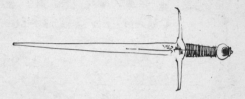

**22. A PANELLED ROOM WITH CARVINGS IN WOOD**

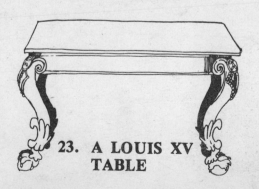

**23. A LOUIS XV TABLE**

**24. A HAT WORN AT THE TIME OF CHARLES II (1660-1685)**

**25. A STAG'S HEAD**

**26. A WEDGWOOD VASE**

**27. A MUSKET**

**28. A CARRIAGE CLOCK**

105

## 29. A CANNON

## 30. AN ORNAMENTAL FOUNTAIN —WITH WATER COMING OUT OF IT!

## 31. A PORTRAIT OF OLIVER CROMWELL

## 32. A DOCUMENT WITH A SEAL ATTACHED TO IT

## 33. A TAPESTRY

## 35. A DOLL'S HOUSE

## 34. A HIDDEN PASSAGE

## 36. A WARMING PAN

## 39. A CLAVICHORD

## 38. A PIKE

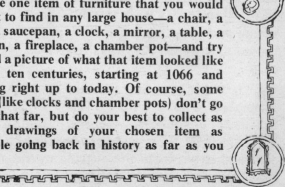

Choose one item of furniture that you would expect to find in any large house—a chair, a bed, a saucepan, a clock, a mirror, a table, a curtain, a fireplace, a chamber pot—and try to find a picture of what that item looked like across ten centuries, starting at 1066 and coming right up to today. Of course, some items (like clocks and chamber pots) don't go back that far, but do your best to collect as many drawings of your chosen item as possible going back in history as far as you can.

THE TOWER OF LONDON

# TOPIARY

Topiary is the art of clipping shrubs and hedges into special shapes. In a number of the gardens of historic houses you will see entertaining examples of topiary: hedges and bushes cut into unusual and interesting shapes. In the gardens of a few great houses, you will also come across mazes made out of shrubbery. Finding your way from the outside of the maze to the inside and then from the centre of the maze back to the outside again is always fun, even if it isn't always easy.

The world's most famous maze is the one at **Hampton Court,** created for William III by his favourite gardeners, George London and Henry Wise, in 1690. The maze covers about a quarter of an acre and to get from the outside to the inside you will have to walk just over half a mile—unless, of course, you try getting from the outside to the inside of this drawing of the Hampton Court maze, in which case you will only have to travel an inch or two:

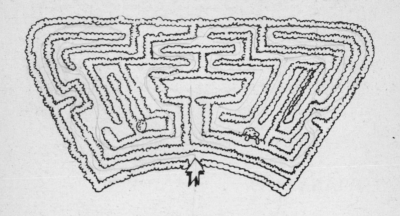

At **Somerleyton Hall** in Suffolk there is another fine garden maze that you can walk through. It was designed and planted in 1846 and if you take no wrong turnings as you travel through it you will walk just four hundred yards from the outside to the centre. If you take a few wrong turnings travelling through this drawing of the Somerleyton Hall Maze, it won't matter:

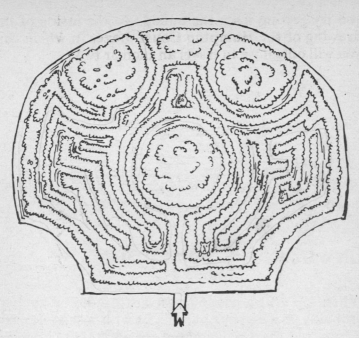

Design your own maze. It looks easy, but it isn't. You will need plenty of rough paper and lots of patience, but if you can design a maze like the ones at Hampton Court and Somerleyton Hall it will have been a job worth doing.

URQUHART CASTLE

## UNWILLINGLY TO SCHOOL

When you visit a castle or an historic home you will probably go with your parents or with a school party. A hundred years ago there were no 'school parties', very few 'outings' and even fewer 'treats'. Children crept unwillingly to school because it was a much stricter place than it is today.

For example, while the younger children were chanting their tables, the older ones were trying to do sums like these:

**The number of art schools in the United Kingdom in 1860 was seventy-eight, and the persons instructed eighty-four thousand and eighty-two; what was the average number of students for each school?**

**A single cod-fish has been found to contain nine millions three hundred and forty-four thousand eggs; how many eggs would there be in one hundred and seventy-four such fish?**

Why don't you try them?
And be sure you get them right,
because if you get them wrong you
may have to sit in the corner wearing
the dunce's cap!

Victorian children had to learn many of their lessons
by heart. Try to learn this poem and this part of a
Geography lesson:

## OBEDIENCE TO PARENTS

LET children that would fear the LORD,
    Hear what their teachers say;
With reverence meet their parents' word,
    And with delight obey.

Have you not heard what dreadful plagues
    Are threatened by the LORD,
To him that breaks his father's law,
    Or mocks his mother's word?

What heavy guilt upon him lies!
    How cursed is his name!
The ravens shall pick out his eyes,
    And eagles eat the same.

But those who worship GOD, and give
    Their parents honour due,
Here on this earth they long shall live,
    And live hereafter too.

Q. Of what shape is the Earth?

A. It is nearly round.

Q. How do you know that?

A. Because ships have sailed round it.

Q. Do you mean that it is like a round table?

A. No; like a ball.

Q. Why, then, do we not fall off as it turns round?

A. Because the earth acts upon us as loadstone does upon steel, and keeps us so close we cannot leave it.

Q. How is the surface divided?

A. Into land and water.

After learning to form letters on slates with special slate pencils, children had to practise writing in copybooks like this, using steel-nib pens. Take care not to 'blot your copybook'.

*Elementary Education Act*

In Drawing lessons children had to copy shapes and patterns carefully.
Try drawing this one:

Visit the local library and find a school textbook that is at least fifty years old. Make sure it is one that was used by children of your own age. When you have found one try some of the exercises in it. If you can't do them, don't worry; at least nowadays you won't be caned for not doing your schoolwork well.

A B C D E F G H I J K L M N O P Q R S T U V W X Y N

V

ST. BRIAVELS CASTLE

# VIZORS UP!

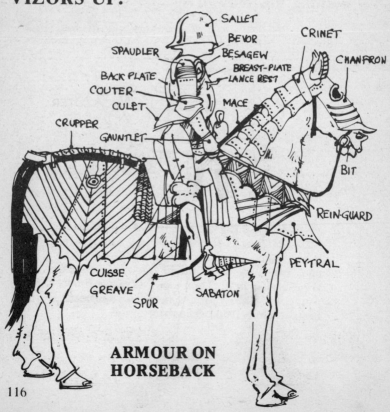

SALLET
BEVOR
SPAUDLER
BESAGEW
BACK PLATE
BREAST-PLATE
LANCE REST
COUTER
CULET
CRUPPER
GAUNTLET
MACE
CRINET
CHANFRON
BIT
REIN-GUARD
PEYTRAL
CUISSE
GREAVE
SPUR
SABATON

## ARMOUR ON
## HORSEBACK

Violence has played its part in the history of most of Britain's castles and great houses. Fortunately, life in England today is much more peaceable than it has been in the past, but when you see a suit of armour on display remember that it was once worn by a real man who had to fight other real men and often fight to the death.

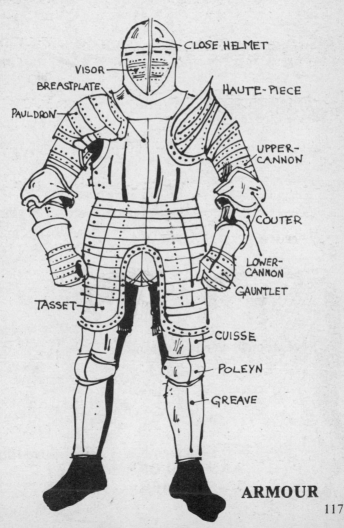

CLOSE HELMET
VISOR
BREASTPLATE
PAULDRON
HAUTE-PIECE
UPPER-CANNON
COUTER
LOWER-CANNON
GAUNTLET
TASSET
CUISSE
POLEYN
GREAVE

**ARMOUR**

117

The castles and historic houses that have collections of weapons usually keep them in what is called an 'armoury'. There are four main categories of weapon:

## THE 'ARME BLANCHE'

**Fifteenth century sword**

**Sixteenth century rapier**

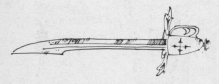

**Seventeenth century sword**

**Fourteenth and fifteenth century Rondel dagger**

# THE ARMS OF PERCUSSION

**The club**

**The mace**

**The flail**

## STAFF WEAPONS

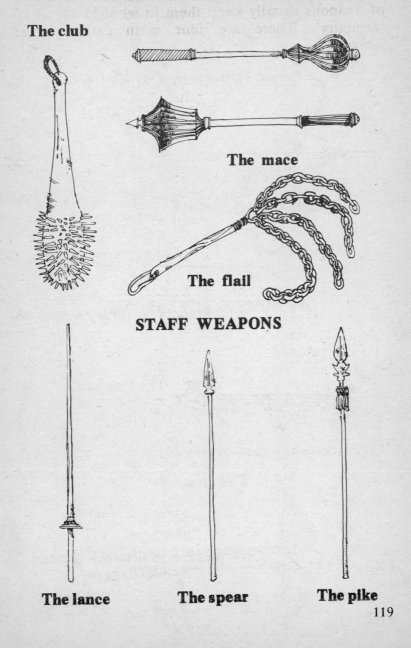

**The lance**          **The spear**          **The pike**

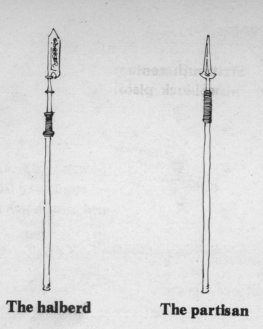

**The halberd**          **The partisan**

## PROJECTILE WEAPONS

**The javelin**

**The longbow**

**The crossbow**

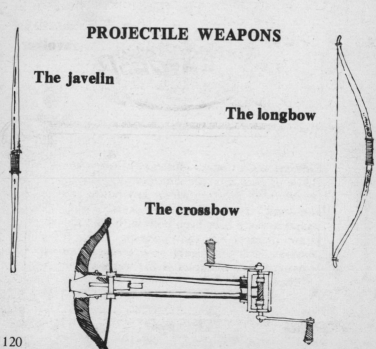

**Sixteenth century
wheel-lock pistol**

**Seventeenth century
combined flint
and matchlock pistol**

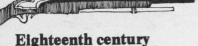

**Eighteenth century
'Brown Bess' musket**

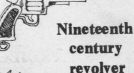

**Nineteenth
century
revolver**

Pick one of the famous battles of history—*the
Battle of Hastings, the Battle of Agincourt,
the Battle of Marston Moor,* any battle you
like—and try to find out exactly what
weapons would have been used in that battle.
Draw pictures of the weapons and, if
possible, visit a museum or a castle or an
armoury where examples of the weapons are
on display today.

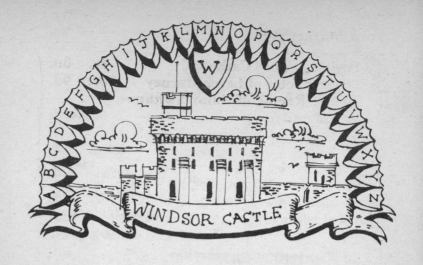

## WHERE THERE'S A WILL

The first Lord Marney died in 1523. He was the man for whom the magnificent **Layer Marney Tower** was built, near Colchester in Essex. In his Will Lord Marney made some interesting bequests.

Wills are fascinating documents and many of the wills of the past owners of great houses and castles are on display. By studying the wills you can learn something about the men themselves and the very different world in which they lived.

## Lord Marney's Will

| | | |
|---|---|---|
| To Saint Paul's Cathedral | 6s. | 8d. |
| To the Rector of Layer Marney | 20s. | 0d. |
| To the Rector of Saint Swithuns, London | 6s. | 8d. |
| To the friars who conveyed his body out of London | 20s. | 0d. each |
| To the churches meeting his body | 3s. | 4d. |
| To the churches resting his body | 6s. | 8d. |
| To 24 'pore men' bearing torches | | 12d. each and a black gown |
| To 30 priests at the burying | | 8d. each |
| To every singing child | | 2d. |
| To the poor—£20 in '1d and 2d doles' | | |
| To all the household servants—one year's wages | | |
| To every archer—a bow and a sheaf of arrows | | |

PROJECT!

Decimal currency was introduced to Britain in 1971. Before then the £ was divided into twenty shillings ('s' for short) and every shilling was divided into twelve pennies ('d.' for short). By reading books like R. J. Unstead's *Looking at History* series, try to find out what you could buy in the past and how much money was then worth.

HURSTMONCEUX CASTLE

## X EQUALS TEN

With Roman numerals **X** equals **10**. **X** is one of the seven basic symbols that make up the Roman system of counting. Here are all seven:

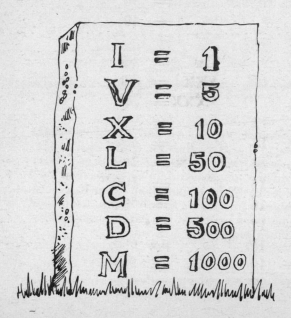

I = 1
V = 5
X = 10
L = 50
C = 100
D = 500
M = 1000

When you see a symbol with another symbol of lower value in front of it, the lower one is subtracted from the greater one to give the total. For example, **IV =** **5 minus 1 = 4** and **CD = 500 minus 100 = 400.** If a symbol is followed by another symbol of the same value or of a smaller value, the symbols are added together to form the total, For example, **VI = 5 plus** **1 = 6** and **XIII = 10 plus 1 plus 1 plus 1 =** **13** and **DC = 500 plus 100 = 600.**

Here is a fuller table to give you a better idea of the way the system of Roman numerals works:

| | | | | | |
|---|---|---|---|---|---|
| I | = 1 | XXI | = 21 | CM | = 900 |
| II | = 2 | XXII | = 22 | M | = 1000 |
| III | = 3 | XXIII | = 23 | MD | = 1500 |
| IV | = 4 | XXIV | = 24 | MCM | = 1900 |
| V | = 5 | XXV | = 25 | MM | = 2000 |
| VI | = 6 | XXX | = 30 | | |
| VII | = 7 | XL | = 40 | | |
| VIII | = 8 | L | = 50 | | |
| IX | = 9 | LX | = 60 | | |
| X | = 10 | LXX | = 70 | | |
| XI | = 11 | LXXX | = 80 | | |
| XII | = 12 | XC | = 90 | | |
| XIII | = 13 | C | = 100 | | |
| XIV | = 14 | CC | = 200 | | |
| XV | = 15 | CCC | = 300 | | |
| XVI | = 16 | CD | = 400 | | |
| XVII | = 17 | D | = 500 | | |
| XVIII | = 18 | DC | = 600 | | |
| XIX | = 19 | DCC | = 700 | | |
| XX | = 20 | DCCC | = 800 | | |

You will often see Roman numerals used in castles and historic houses, so they are well worth learning. To find out how much you already know, see if you can decipher the numbers here:

1.

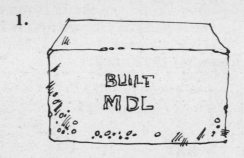

BUILT
MDL

2.

CHARLES II
MDCLX - MDCLXXXV

**3.**

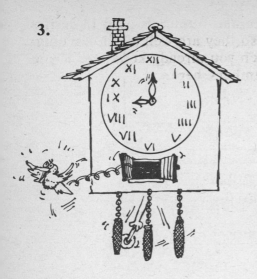

What time is it ?
(Note that on clocks
the **IV** is sometimes
written as **IIII**)

**4.**

Queen
Victoria's
Diamond
Jubilee
MCCMXCVII

**5.**

RICHARD III

MCDLXXXIII - MCDLXXXV

**6.**

HERITAGE
EDUCATION
YEAR.

MCMLXXVII

Make a portrait gallery of all the Kings and Queens of England from William the Conqueror in 1066 to Elizabeth II today. Get a picture from a book or a postcard or a photograph of each monarch and stick them into an album in the right order. If you cannot find an authentic portrait, draw one of your own. Underneath each picture, put the monarch's name and dates—in Roman numerals, of course!

## YOUR FAVOURITE

Of all the castles and historic houses in England, Wales, Scotland and Ireland, which is your favourite? Is it **Sudeley Castle** in the Cotswolds? Is it **Scone Palace** in Perth? Is it **Sledmere House** in Yorkshire? Is it **Brympton d'Evercy** in Somerset? Is it **Castle Ashby** near Northampton? Is it **Cameron House** on Loch Lomond? Is it **Castletown House** in County Kildare? Is it **Cardiff Castle**? Is it **Warwick Castle**? Is it **Windsor Castle**? Which one of the hundreds you can choose from is *your* favourite?

When you have decided which it is, let us know. This is the information we would like you to send us:

THE NAME OF YOUR FAVOURITE CASTLE OR HISTORIC HOUSE

ITS ADDRESS

THE DATE YOU VISITED IT

THE REASON IT IS YOUR FAVOURITE

129

YOUR NAME

YOUR ADDRESS

YOUR DATE OF BIRTH

And this is where you should send your vote:

Gyles Brandreth
PROJECT: CASTLES & HISTORIC
    HOUSES
Transworld Publishers
Century House
61-63 Uxbridge Road, LONDON W5 5SA

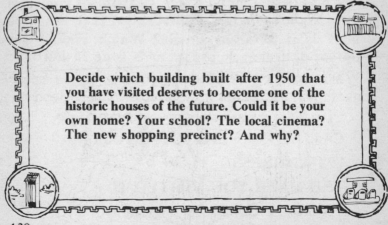

Decide which building built after 1950 that you have visited deserves to become one of the historic houses of the future. Could it be your own home? Your school? The local cinema? The new shopping precinct? And why?

LOCHRANZA CASTLE

## ZZZZZ

Time for bed! And here are just a few of the beds you might have slept in had you lived in the past instead of today.

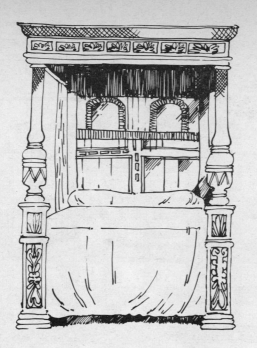

Take a good look at the list of historic houses, castles and gardens that starts over the page. Decide which ones you would like to visit this year. Make a list of them—and then try to persuade your parents or your teachers (or both!) to take you to visit them.

# ANSWERS

## HEROES OF HISTORY

1. Ann Boleyn
2. William Shakespeare
3. The Duke of Wellington
4. George Washington
5. Sir Walter Raleigh
6. Florence Nightingale
7. Sir Winston Churchill
8. Beatrix Potter
9. Benjamin Disraeli
10. Macbeth

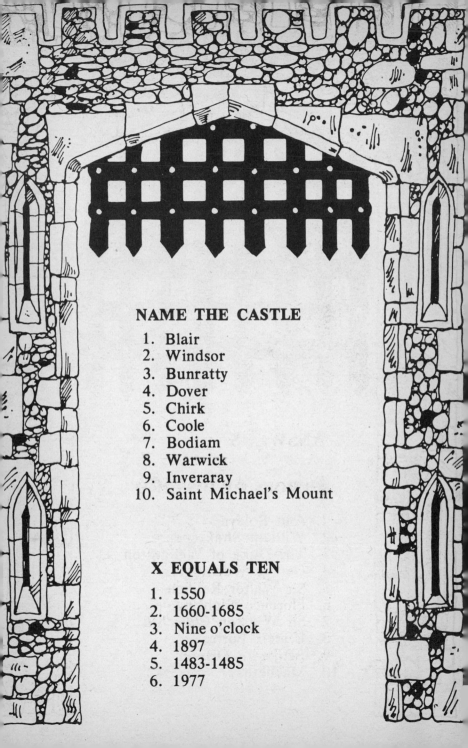

## NAME THE CASTLE

1. Blair
2. Windsor
3. Bunratty
4. Dover
5. Chirk
6. Coole
7. Bodiam
8. Warwick
9. Inveraray
10. Saint Michael's Mount

## X EQUALS TEN

1. 1550
2. 1660-1685
3. Nine o'clock
4. 1897
5. 1483-1485
6. 1977

Every dot on the map marks the spot where you will find a fascinating historic building. As you can see, there are plenty to choose from. On the next nine pages are listed the names of the historic houses, castles and gardens in the United Kingdom and Ireland which are open to the public. They are given county by county, so you shouldn't find it difficult to find some near you. Your parents, your teachers or you will have to find out for yourselves exactly when each house is open and how much (if anything) it costs to visit.

## AVON

| | |
|---|---|
| Badminton House. | Badminton. |
| Blaise Castle House. | Henbury. |
| Claverton Manor. | Nr. Bath. |
| Clevedon Court. | Nr. Clevedon. |
| Dodington House. | Chipping Sodbury. |
| Dyrham Park. | Nr. Bristol and Bath. |
| Georgian House (1790). | Bristol. |
| Horton Court. | Horton. |
| Little Sodbury Manor. | Chipping Sodbury. |
| Red Lodge. | Bristol. |
| No. 1 Royal Crescent. | Bath. |
| St. Vincent's Priory. | Clifton. |
| Vine House. | Henbury. |

## BEDFORDSHIRE.

| | |
|---|---|
| Luton Hoo. | Luton. |
| Stagsden Bird Gardens. | Stagsden. |
| Woburn Abbey and Wild Animal Kingdom. | Woburn. |
| Wrest Park. | Silsoe. |

## BERKSHIRE.

| | |
|---|---|
| No. 25 The Cloisters. | Windsor Castle. |
| The Old Rectory. | Burghfield. |
| Savill Garden. | Windsor Great Park. |
| Swallowfield Park. | Swallowfield. |
| Valley Gardens. | Windsor Great Park. |
| Wexham Springs. | Wexham. |
| Windsor Castle. | Windsor. |

| | |
|---|---|
| Bodiam Castle. | Nr. Hawkhurst. |
| Brickwall House. | Northiam, Rye. |
| Charleston Manor. | Westdean, Seaford. |
| Durbar Hall. | Hastings. |
| Firle Place. | Nr. Lewes. |
| Glynde Place. | Nr. Lewes. |
| Great Dixter. | Northiam. |
| Haremere Hall. | Etchingham. |
| Horsted Place Gardens. | Nr. Uckfield. |
| Kidbrooke Park. | Forest Row. |
| Lamb House. | Rye. |
| Michelham Priory. | Nr. Hailsham. |
| The Old Minthouse. | Pevensey. |
| Preston Manor. | Brighton. |
| Royal Pavilion. | Brighton. |
| Sheffield Park. | Nr. Uckfield. |
| Sheffield Park Garden. | Nr. Uckfield. |
| The Spring Hill Wildfowl Park. | Forest Row. |
| Standen. | East Grinstead. |

## BUCKINGHAMSHIRE.

| | |
|---|---|
| Ascott. | Wing. |
| Boarstall Duck Decoy. | Nr. Brill. |
| Chicheley Hall. | Newport Pagnell. |
| Claydon House. | Middle Claydon, Nr. Winslow. |
| Cliveden. | Maidenhead. |
| Hartwell House. | Aylesbury. |
| Hughenden Manor. | High Wycombe. |
| The Manor House. | Chenies. |
| Milton Cottage. | Chalfont St. Giles. |
| Nether Winchendon House. | Aylesbury. |
| Stearthill. | Little Horwood. |
| Stowe School. | Buckingham. |
| Waddesden Manor. | Nr. Aylesbury. |
| West Wycombe Park (1750). | West Wycombe. |
| Wootton House. | Nr. Aylesbury. |

## CAMBRIDGESHIRE.

| | |
|---|---|
| Anglesey Abbey. | Nr. Cambridge. |
| Hinchingbrooke House. | Huntingdon. |
| Kimbolton Castle. | Kimbolton. |
| The King's School. | Ely. |
| Northborough Castle. | Northborough. |
| Peckover House. | Wisbech. |
| University Botanic Garden. | Cambridge. |

138

## CHESHIRE.

| | |
|---|---|
| Adlington Hall. | Macclesfield. |
| Arley Hall Gardens. | Northwich. |
| Capesthorne. | Macclesfield. |
| Cholmondeley Castle Gardens. | Malpas. |
| Chorley Old Hall. | Alderley Edge. |
| Churche's Mansion. | Nantwich. |
| Dorfold Hall. | Nantwich. |
| Gawsworth Hall. | Macclesfield. |
| Little Moreton Hall. | Congleton. |
| Lyme Park. | Disley. |
| Nether Alderley Mill. | Nether Alderley. |
| Norton Priory Museum. | Runcorn. |
| Peover Hall. | Over Peoford, Knutsford. |
| Tatton Park. | Knutsford. |

## CLEVELAND.

| | |
|---|---|
| Ormesby Hall. | Nr. Middlesbrough. |

## CORNWALL.

| | |
|---|---|
| Antony House. | Torpoint. |
| Cotehele House. | Calstock. |
| Ebbingford Manor. | Bude. |
| Glendurgan Garden. | Helford River. |
| Godolphin House. | Helston. |
| Lanhydrock. | Near Bodmin. |
| Mount Edgcumbe. | Nr. Plymouth. |
| Pencarrow House & Gardens. | Bodmin. |
| Pendennis Castle. | Falmouth. |
| St. Michael's Mount. | Penzance. |
| Tintagel, Old Post Office. | Tintagel. |
| Tresselissick Garden. | Near Truro. |
| Tremeer. | St. Tudy. |
| Trengwainton Garden. | Penzance. |
| Trerice. | St. Newlyn East. |
| Trewithen. | Probus, Nr. Truro. |

## CUMBRIA.

| | |
|---|---|
| Abbot Hall Art Gallery & Museum of Lakeland Life & Industry. | Kendal. |
| Acorn Bank. | Temple Sowerby. |
| Belle Isle. | Bowness-on-Windermere. |
| Carlisle Castle. | Carlisle. |
| Dalemain. | Nr. Penrith. |
| Graythwaite Hall. | Ulverston. |

| | |
|---|---|
| Molker Hall. | Cark-in-Cartmel. |
| Hutton-in-the-Forest. | Penrith. |
| Levens Hall. | Kendal. |
| Lingholm. | Keswick. |
| Muncaster Castle. | Ravenglass. |
| Rydal Mount. | Ambleside. |
| Sizergh Castle. | Kendal. |
| Stagshaw. | Ambleside. |
| Townend. | Troutbeck. |
| Whitehall. | Mealsgate. |
| Wordsworth House. | Cockermouth. |

## DERBYSHIRE.

| | |
|---|---|
| Chatsworth. | Bakewell. |
| Ednaston Manor. | Brailsford. |
| Foremarke Hall. | Milton. |
| Haddon Hall. | Bakewell. |
| Hardwick Hall. | Nr. Chesterfield. |
| Kedleston Hall. | Derby. |
| Lea Rhododendron Gardens. | Lea. |
| Melbourne Hall. | Melbourne. |
| The Old House Museum. | Bakewell. |
| Sudbury Hall. | Nr. Derby. |
| Winster Market House. | Nr. Matlock. |

## DEVONSHIRE.

| | |
|---|---|
| Arlington Court. | Barnstaple. |
| Bickham House. | Roborough. |
| Bickleigh Castle. | Nr. Tiverton. |
| Bradley Manor. | Newton Abbot. |
| Buckland Abbey. | Nr. Plymouth. |
| Cadhay. | Ottery St. Mary. |
| Castle Crogo. | Nr. Chagford. |
| Castle Hill. | Filleigh, Barnstaple. |
| Chambercombe Manor. | Ilfracombe. |
| Combe Head. | Bampton. |
| Compton Castle. | Nr. Paignton. |
| Dartmouth Castle. | Dartmouth. |
| Flete. | Ermington, Ivybridge. |
| The Garden House. | Buckland Monachorum, Yelverton. |
| Killerton Garden. | Nr. Exeter. |
| Kirkham House. | Paignton. |
| Knightshayes Court. | Nr. Tiverton. |
| Lee Ford. | Budleigh Salterton. |
| Marwood Hill. | Nr. Barnstaple. |
| Powderham Castle. | Nr. Exeter. |

| | |
|---|---|
| Rosemoor Garden Charitable Trust. | Torrington. |
| Saltram House. | Plymouth. |
| Charpitor. | Salcombe. |
| Tapeley Park Gardens. | Instow. |
| Tiverton Castle. | Nr. Tiverton. |

## DORSET.

| | |
|---|---|
| Athelhampton. | Athelhampton. |
| Clouds Hill. | Nr. Wareham. |
| Compton Acres Gardens. | Poole, Nr. Bournemouth. |
| Cranborne Manor Gardens. | Wimborne. |
| Dewlish House. | Dewlish. |
| Forde Abbey. | Nr. Chard. |
| Hardy's Cottage. | Higher Bockhampton. |
| Hyde Crook. | Dorchester. |
| The Manor House. | Sandford Orcas. |
| Melbury House. | Nr. Yeovil. |
| Milton Abbey. | Nr. Blandford. |
| Minterne. | Dorchester. |
| Parnham House. | Beaminster. |
| Purse Caundle Manor. | Purse Caundle. |
| Russell-Cotes Art Gallery and Museum. | Bournemouth. |
| Sherborne Castle. | Sherborne. |
| Smedmore. | Kimmeridge. |
| No. 3 Trinity Street. | Weymouth. |
| Wolfeton House. | Dorchester. |

## DURHAM.

| | |
|---|---|
| The Bowes Museum. | Barnard Castle. |
| Durham Castle. | Durham. |
| Raby Castle. | Staindrop, Darlington. |

## EAST SUSSEX.

| | |
|---|---|
| Alfriston Clergy House. | Nr. Seaford. |
| Bateman's. | Burwash. |
| Battle Abbey. | Battle. |
| Beeches Farm. | Nr. Uckfield. |
| Bentley. | Halland, Nr. Lewes. |
| Bodiam Castle. | Nr. Hawkhurst. |
| Brickwall House. | Northiam, Rye. |
| Charleston Manor. | Westdean, Seaford. |
| Durbar Hall. | Hastings. |
| Firle Place. | Nr. Lewes. |
| Glynde Place. | Nr Lewes. |

141

| | |
|---|---|
| Great Dixter. | Northiam. |
| Haremere Hall. | Etchingham. |
| Horsted Place Gardens. | Nr. Uckfield. |
| Kidbrooke Park. | Forest Row. |
| Lamb House. | Rye. |
| Michelham Priory. | Nr. Hailsham. |
| The Old Minthouse. | Pevensey. |
| Preston Manor. | Brighton. |
| Royal Pavillion. | Brighton. |
| Sheffield Park. | Nr. Uckfield. |
| Sheffield Park Garden. | Nr. Uckfield. |
| The Spring Hill Wildfowl Park. | Forest Row. |
| Standen. | East Grinstead. |

## ESSEX.

| | |
|---|---|
| Audley End House. | Saffron Walden. |
| Blue Bridge House. | Halstead. |
| Castle House. | Dedham. |
| Gosfield Hall. | Halstead. |
| Hedingham Castle. | Castle Hedingham. |
| Ingatestone Hall. | Ingatestone. |
| Layer Marney Tower. | Nr. Colchester. |
| Paycocke's. | Coggeshall. |
| White Barn House. | Elmstead Market. |

## GLOUCESTERSHIRE.

| | |
|---|---|
| Arlington Mill. | Bibury. |
| Barnsley House Garden. | Barnsley. |
| Barnsley Park. | Cirencester. |
| Batsford Park Arboretum. | Moreton-in-Marsh. |
| Berkeley Castle. | Nr. Bristol. |
| Buckland Rectory. | Nr. Broadway. |
| Chavenage. | Tetbury. |
| Clearwell Castle. | Nr. Coleford. |
| Court House. | Painswick. |
| Hidcote Manor Garden. | Nr. Chipping Campden. |
| Kilmscott Manor. | Nr. Lechlade. |
| Kiftsgate Court. | Nr. Chipping Camden. |
| Lydney Park. | Lydney. |
| Misarden Park. | Nr. Stroud. |
| Snowshill Manor. | Broadway. |
| Sudeley Castle. | Winchcombe. |
| Upper Slaughter Manor House. | Cheltenham. |
| Westbury Court Garden. | Westbury-on-Severn. |
| Westonbirt Arboretum. | Tetbury. |

## GREATER MANCHESTER.

| | |
|---|---|
| Fletcher Moss. | Didsbury. |
| Heaton Hall. | Heaton Park, Prestwich. |
| Newton Hall. | Hyde. |
| Platt Hall. | Platt Fields, Rusholme. |
| Wythenshawe Hall. | Northenden. |

## HAMPSHIRE.

| | |
|---|---|
| Avington Park. | Winchester. |
| Beaulieu Abbey and Palace House,<br>  National Motor Museum. | Beaulieu. |
| Breamore House. | Nr. Fordingbridge. |
| Furzey Gardens. | Minstead, Nr. Lyndhurst. |
| Grove Place. | Nursling, Southampton. |
| Hurst Mill. | Petersfield. |
| Jane Austen's Home. | Chawton. |
| Jenkyn Place. | Bentley. |
| Mottisfont Abbey. | Mottisfont. |
| The Pilgrims' Hall. | Winchester. |
| Sandham Memorial Chapel. | Nr. Newbury. |
| Spinners. | Boldre. |
| Stratfield Saye House. | Reading. |
| The Vyne. | Basingstoke. |
| West Green House. | Hartley Wintney. |

## HEREFORD & WORCESTER.

| | |
|---|---|
| Abbey Dore Court Garden. | Nr. Hereford. |
| Avoncroft Museum of Buildings. | Nr. Bromsgrove. |
| Berrington Hall. | Leominster. |
| Brilley, Cwmmau Farmhouse. | Whitney-on-Wye. |
| Broadway Tower Country Park. | Broadway. |
| Burton Court. | Eardisland. |
| Croft Castle. | Nr. Leominster. |
| Dinmore Manor. | Nr. Hereford. |
| Eastnor Castle. | Nr. Ledbury. |
| Eye Manor. | Leominster. |
| The Greyfriars. | Worcester. |
| Hanbury Hall. | Nr. Droitwich. |
| Harvington Hall. | Kidderminster. |
| Hellen's. | Much Marcle. |
| Hergest Croft Garden &<br>  Park Wood. | Kington. |
| Little Malvern Court. | Nr. Gt. Malvern. |
| Lower Brockhampton. | Bromyard. |
| Moccas Court. | Moccas. |
| Pembridge Castle. | Welsh Newton. |
| Spetchey Park. | Worcester. |
| The Weir. | Swainshill. |

## HERTFORDSHIRE.

| | |
|---|---|
| Ashridge. | Berkhamsted. |
| Gorhambury House. | St. Albans. |
| Hatfield House. | Hatfield. |
| Knebworth House. | Knebworth. |
| Moor Park Mansion. | Moor Park. |
| Piccotts End Medieval Wall Paintings. | Nr. Hemel Hempstead. |
| Salisbury Hall. | London Colney. |
| Shaw's Corner. | Ayot St. Lawrence. |

## HUMBERSIDE.

| | |
|---|---|
| Blaydes House. | Hull. |
| Burnby Hall Gardens. | Pocklington. |
| Burton Agnes Hall. | Bridlington. |
| Burton Constable. | Nr. Hull. |
| Elsham Hall, Country Park and Creative Centre. | Brigg. |
| Epworth—The Old Rectory. | Epworth. |
| Maister House. | Hull. |
| Normanby Hall. | Scunthorpe. |
| Sewerby Hall. | Bridlington. |
| Sledmere House. | Driffield. |
| Wilberforce House. | Hull. |

## ISLE OF WIGHT.

| | |
|---|---|
| Arreton Manor. | Arreton. |
| Carisbrooke Castle. | Nr. Newport. |
| Newtown Old Town Hall. | Newtown. |
| Nunwell House. | Brading. |
| Osborne House. | East Cowes. |

## KENT.

| | |
|---|---|
| Allington Castle. | Nr. Maidstone. |
| Aylesford—The Friars. | Aylesford. |
| Bedgebury Pinetum. | Nr. Goudhurst. |
| Black Charles. | Nr. Sevenoaks. |
| Boughton Monchelsea Place. | Nr. Maidstone. |
| Chartwell. | Westerham. |
| Chiddingstone Castle. | Nr. Edenbridge. |
| Chilham Castle. | Nr. Canterbury. |
| Cobham Hall. | Cobham. |
| Crittenden House. | Matfield. |
| Deal Castle. | Deal. |
| Dover Castle. | Dover. |
| Down House. | Downe. |
| Emmetts Garden. | Nr. Brasted. |
| Eyhorne Manor. | Hollingbourne. |

144

| | |
|---|---|
| Finchcocks. | Goudhurst. |
| Godington Park. | Ashford. |
| Great Comp. | Nr. Borough Green. |
| Great Maytham Hall. | Rolvenden. |
| Hever Castle. | Nr. Edenbridge. |
| Hole Park. | Rolvenden. |
| Ian Ramsey College, Brasted Place. | Nr. Westerham. |
| Ightman Mote. | Ivy Hatch. |
| Knole. | Sevenoaks. |
| Ladham House. | Goudhurst. |
| Leeds Castle. | Nr. Maidstone. |
| Lullingstone Castle. | Eynsford. |
| Lympne Castle. | Nr. Hythe. |
| Old Soar Manor. | Nr. Borough Green. |
| Owletts. | Cobham. |
| The Owl House. | Lamberhurst. |
| Pattydene Manor. | Goudhurst. |
| Penshurst Place. | Tunbridge Wells. |
| Quebec House. | Westerham. |
| St. John's Jerusalem Garden. | Dartford. |
| Saltwood Castle. | Nr. Hythe. |
| Sandling Park. | Nr. Hythe. |
| Scotney Castle Garden. | Lamberhurst. |
| Sissinghurst Castle. | Sissinghurst. |
| Sissinghurst Court. | Cranbrook. |
| Smallhythe Place. | Tenterden. |
| Squerryes Court. | Westerham. |
| Stoneacre. | Otham. |
| Swanton Mill. | Mersham. |
| Temple Manor. | Rochester. |
| Walmer Castle. | Walmer. |
| Warden Manor. | Isle of Sheppey. |

## LANCASHIRE.

| | |
|---|---|
| Astley Hall. | Chorley. |
| Chingle Hall. | Goosnargh, Nr. Preston. |
| Cranford. | Aughton. |
| Gawthorpe Hall. | Padiham. |
| Leighton Hall. | Carnforth. |
| Martholme Gatehouse. | Great Harwood. |
| Ravenhurst. | Bolton. |
| Rufford Old Hall. | Rufford. |
| Towneley Hall Art Gallery & Museum of Local Crafts & Industries. | Burnley. |
| Windle Hall. | St. Helen's. |

145

## LEICESTERSHIRE.

| | |
|---|---|
| Belgrave Hall. | Leicester. |
| Belvoir Castle. | Nr. Grantham. |
| Guildhall. | Leicester. |
| Langton Hall. | Nr. Market Harborough. |
| Manor House. | Donington le Heath. |
| Oakham Castle. | Oakham. |
| Prestwold Hall. | Loughborough. |
| Quenby Hall. | Hungarton. |
| Stanford Hall. | Lutterworth. |
| Stapleford Park. | Nr. Melton Mowbray. |
| Wygston's House. | Leicester. |

## LINCOLNSHIRE.

| | |
|---|---|
| Aubourn Hall. | Nr. Lincoln. |
| Belton House. | Grantham. |
| Doddington Hall. | Doddington. |
| Fydell House. | Boston. |
| Grantham House. | Grantham. |
| Gunby Hall. | Burgh-le-Marsh. |
| Marston Hall. | Grantham. |
| The Old Hall. | Gainsborough. |
| Tattershall Castle (1440). | Lincoln. |
| Woolsthorpe Manor. | Nr. Grantham. |

## LONDON.

| | |
|---|---|
| Apsley House. | Wellington Museum. |
| Arkley Manor. | Nr. Barnet. |
| Ashburnham House. | Westminster. |
| Boston Manor House. | Brentford. |
| Carlyle's House. | Chelsea. |
| Chiswick House. | Chiswick. |
| Eastbury Manor House. | Barking. |
| Fenton House. | Hampstead. |
| Forty Hall. | Enfield. |
| Hall Place. | Bexley. |
| Ham House. | Richmond. |
| Hampton Court Palace. | Hampton Court. |
| Hogarth's House. | Chiswick. |
| Iveagh Bequest. | Kenwood. |
| Keats House. | Hampstead. |
| Kensington Palace. | Kensington. |
| Kew Gardens. | Kew. |
| Kew Palace. | Kew (Dutch House). |
| Lancaster House. | Nr. St. James's. |
| Marble Hill House. | Twickenham. |
| Marlborough House. | Pall Mall. |
| The Old Palace. | Croydon. |

| | |
|---|---|
| Old Royal Observatory. | Greenwich. |
| Orleans House Gallery. | Riverside. |
| Osterley Park House. | Osterley. |
| The Queen's House. | Greenwich. |
| Rangers House. | Blackheath. |
| Royal Naval College. | Greenwich. |
| Syon House. | Brentford. |
| Syon Park Gardens. | Brentford. |
| Tower of London. | Tower Bridge. |
| White Lodge. | Richmond Park. |

## MERSEYSIDE.

| | |
|---|---|
| Speke Hall. | Liverpool. |

## NORFOLK.

| | |
|---|---|
| Blickling Hall. | Aylsham.Caister Castle. |
| Felbrigg Hall. | Nr. Cromer. |
| Fritton Lake & Gardens. | Norfolk. |
| Holkham Hall. | Wells. |
| Oxburgh Hall. | Swaffham. |
| Sandringham Grounds. | Sandringham. |
| Trinity Hospital. | Castle Rising. |
| Walsingham Abbey. | Walsingham. |
| Wolterton Hall. | Nr. Norwich. |

## NORTHAMPTONSHIRE.

| | |
|---|---|
| Althorp. | Northampton. |
| Aynhoe Park. | Aynho. |
| Boughton House. | Kettering. |
| Burghley House. | Stamford. |
| Castle Ashby. | Northampton. |
| Coton Manor Wildlife Garden. | Nr. Rugby. |
| Cotterstock Hall. | Nr. Peterborough. |
| Deene Park. | Nr. Corby. |
| Delapre Abbey. | Nr. Northampton. |
| Guilsborough Grange Bird & Pet Park. | Guilsborough. |
| Hinwick House. | Nr. Wellingborough. |
| Kirby Hall. | Gretton. |
| Lamport Hall. | Northampton. |
| Lyveden New Bield. | Oundle. |
| Priest's House. | Easton-on-the-Hill. |
| Rockingham Castle. | Nr. Corby. |
| Southwick Hall. | Nr. Oundle. |
| Stoke Park Pavilions. | Towchester. |
| Sulgrave Manor. | Banbury. |

147

## NORTHUMBERLAND.

| | |
|---|---|
| Alnwick Castle. | Alnwick. |
| Bamburgh Castle. | Bamburgh. |
| Callaly Castle. | Whittingham. |
| Howick Gardens. | Alnwick. |
| Lindisfarne Castle. | Holy Island. |
| Seaton Delaval Hall. | Nr. Newcastle-upon-Tyne. |
| Wallington Hall. | Cambo. |

## NORTH YORKSHIRE.

| | |
|---|---|
| Bedale Hall. | Bedale. |
| Beningbrough Hall. | Nr. Shipton. |
| Brandsby Hall. | York. |
| Broughton Hall. | Skipton. |
| Castle Howard. | York. |
| Duncombe Park. | Helmsley. |
| Fountains Abbey. | Ripon. |
| Georgian Theatre. | Richmond. |
| Gilling Castle. | Helmsley. |
| Jervaulx Abbey. | Nr. Masham. |
| Markenfield Hall. | Ripon. |
| Merchant Adventurers' Hall. | Fossgate, York. |
| Newburgh Priory. | Coxwold. |
| Newby Hall. | Ripon. |
| Norton Conyers. | Ripon. |
| Nunnington Hall. | Ryedale. |
| Foston—The Old Rectory. | Foston. |
| Rievaulx Terrace. | Helmsley. |
| Ripley Castle. | Ripley. |
| Shandy Hall. | Coxwold. |
| Skipton Castle. | Skipton. |
| Sutton Park. | Sutton-on-the-Forest. |
| Treasurer's House. | York. |

## NOTTINGHAMSHIRE.

| | |
|---|---|
| Clumber Chapel. | Clumber Park. |
| Holme Pierrepont Hall. | Radcliffe-on-Trent, Nr. Nottingham. |
| Newstead Abbey. | Linby. |
| Thoresby Hall. | Ollerton. |
| Thrumpton Hall. | Nottingham. |
| Wollaton Hall. | Nottingham. |

## OXFORDSHIRE.

| | |
|---|---|
| Abbey Buildings. | Abingdon. |
| Ashdown House. | Nr. Lambourn. |
| Blenheim Palace. | Woodstock. |
| Botanic Gardens. | Oxford. |
| Broughton Castle. | Banbury. |

| | |
|---|---|
| Buscot Old Parsonage. | Nr. Lechlade. |
| Buscot Park. | Nr. Faringdon. |
| Chastleton House. | Moreton-in-Marsh. |
| Ditchley Park. | Enstone. |
| Edgcote. | Chipping Warden. |
| The Great Barn. | Great Coxwell. |
| Greys Court. | Henley-on-Thames. |
| Hinton Manor. | Hinton Waldrist. |
| Mapledurham House. | Mapledurham. |
| Milton Manor House. | Nr. Abingdon. |
| Nuneham. | Nr. Oxford. |
| Pusey House Gardens. | Nr. Faringdon. |
| Rousham House. | Steeple Aston. |
| Waterperry Horticultural Centre. | Nr. Wheatley. |
| University of Oxford. | Oxford. |

## SHROPSHIRE.

| | |
|---|---|
| Acton Round Hall. | Bridgnorth. |
| Attingham Park. | Nr. Shrewsbury. |
| Benthall Hall. | Much Wenlock. |
| Boscobel House. | Shifnal. |
| Burford House Gardens. | Nr. Tenbury Wells. |
| Hodnet Hall Gardens. | Nr. Market Drayton. |
| Mawley Hall. | Cleobury Mortimer. |
| Shipton Hall. | Much Wenlock. |
| Tyn-y-Rhos Hall. | Nr. Oswestry. |
| Upton Cressett Hall. | Bridgenorth. |
| Wenlock Priory. | Much Wenlock. |
| Weston Park. | Nr. Shifnal. |
| The White House. | Aston Munslow. |
| Wilderhope Manor. | Wenlock Edge. |

## SOMERSET.

| | |
|---|---|
| Barford Park. | Enmore. |
| Barrington Court. | Ilminster. |
| Brympton d'Evercy. | Nr. Yeovil. |
| Coleridge Cottage. | Nether Stowey. |
| Dodington Hall. | Nether Stowey. |
| Dunster Castle. | Dunster. |
| East Lambrook Manor. | South Petherton. |
| Gaulden Manor. | Tolland, Nr. Taunton. |
| Hadspen House. | Castle Cary. |
| Halsway Manor. | Nr. Crowcombe. |
| Hatch Court. | Hatch Beauchamp. |
| King John's Hunting Lodge. | Axbridge. |
| Lytes Cary. | Somerton. |
| Montacute House. | Yeovil. |
| The Palace. | Wells. |

149

| Priest's House. | Muchelney. |
| Stoke-Sub-Hamdon Priory. | Nr. Yeovil. |
| Stowell Hill. | Templecombe. |
| Tintinhull House. | Yeovil. |

## SOUTH YORKSHIRE.

| Cannon Hall. | Cawthorne. |
| Carlton Towers. | Goole. |
| Oakes Park. | Nr. Sheffield. |

## STAFFORDSHIRE.

| Blithfield Hall. | Nr. Rugeley. |
| Chillington Hall. | Nr. Wolverhampton. |
| Elds Wood. | Willoughbridge. |
| Hoar Cross Hall. | Nr. Burton-on-Trent |
| Shugborough. | Stafford. |
| Tamworth Castle. | Tamworth. |
| Trentham Gardens. | Trentham. |
| Weston Park. | Shropshire. |

## SUFFOLK.

| Christchurch Mansion. | Ipswich. |
| Euston Hall. | Thetford. |
| Gainsborough's House. | Sudbury. |
| Glemham Hall. | Nr. Woodbridge. |
| The Guildhall. | Hadleigh. |
| Haughley Park. | Nr. Stowmarket. |
| Helmingham Hall Gardens. | Ipswich. |
| Heveningham Hall. | Nr. Halesworth. |
| Ickworth. | Nr. Bury St. Edmunds. |
| Ixworth Abbey. | Bury St. Edmunds. |
| Kentwell Hill. | Long Melford. |
| Little Hall. | Lavenham. |
| Melford Hall. | Nr. Sudbury. |
| Somerleyton Hall. | Nr. Lowestoft. |

## SURREY.

| Albury Park. | Albury, Guildford. |
| Chilworth Manor. | Nr. Guildford. |
| Clandon Park. | Nr. Guildford. |
| Claremont. | Esher. |
| Detillens. | Limpsfield. |
| Feathercombe Gardens. | Hambledon. |
| Greathed Manor. | Lingfield. |
| Hascombe Court. | Nr. Godalming. |
| Hatchlands. | East Clandon. |
| Loseley House. | Guildford. |
| Polesden Lacey. | Nr. Dorking. |

Ramster.                              Chiddingfold.
Winkworth Arboretum.                  Nr. Godalming.
Wisley Garden.                        Wisley, Ripley.

## TYNE & WEAR.

Gibside Chapel & Avenue.              Gibside.
Washington Old Hall.                  Washington.

## WARWICKSHIRE.

Arbury Hall.                          Nuneaton.
Charlecote Park.                      Warwick.
Compton Wynyates.                     Tysoe.
Coughton Court.                       Alcester.
Farnborough Hall.                     Nr. Banbury.
Harvard House.                        Stratford-upon-Avon.
Kenilworth Castle.                    Kenilworth.
Lord Leycester Hospital.              Warwick.
Packwood House.                       Hockley Heath.
Ragley Hall.                          Alcester.
Shakespeare's Birthplace
  Trust Properties.                   Stratford-upon-Avon.
Upton House.                          Edgehill.
Warwick Castle.                       Warwick.

## WEST MIDLANDS.

Aston Hall.                           Birmingham.
Moseley Old Hall.                     Wolverhampton.
Oak House.                            West Bromwich.
Wightwick Manor.                      Wolverhampton.

## WEST SUSSEX.

Arundel Castle.                       Arundel.
Borde Hill Garden.                    Haywards Heath.
Christ's Hospital.                    Horsham.
Cuckfield Park.                       Cuckfield.
Danny.                                Hurstpierpoint.
Goodwood House.                       Chichester.
Heaselands.                           Haywards Heath.
Leonardslee.                          Horsham.
Newtimber Place.                      Newtimber.
Nymans Garden.                        Handcross.
Parham.                               Pulborough.
Petworth House.                       Petworth.
St. Mary's.                           Bramber.
South Lodge.                          Lower Beeding.
Tanyard.                              Sharpthorne.
The Thatched Cottage.                 Lindfield.
Uppark.                               South Harting, Nr. Petersfield.

Wakehurst Place Garden.    Nr. Ardingly.
The Weald and Downland Open
    Air Museum, Singleton.    Nr. Chichester.

## WEST YORKSHIRE.

| | |
|---|---|
| Ackworth School. | Pontefract. |
| Bolling Hall. | Bradford. |
| Bramham Park. | Wetherby. |
| Bronte Parsonage Museum. | Haworth. |
| East Riddlesden Hall. | Keighley. |
| Harewood House & Bird Garden. | Leeds. |
| Harlow Car Gardens. | Harrogate. |
| Heath Hall. | Nr. Wakefield. |
| Heptonstall Old Grammar School Museum. | Hebden Bridge. |
| Lotherton Hall. | Aberford. |
| Manor House. | Ilkley. |
| Nostell Priory. | Wakefield. |
| Oakwell Hall. | Batley. |
| Parcevall Hall. | Wharfedale. |
| Redhouse. | Cleckheaton. |
| Shibden Hall. | Halifax. |
| Temple Museum. | Leeds. |

## WILTSHIRE.

| | |
|---|---|
| Bowood Gardens. | Calne. |
| Broadleas. | Devizes. |
| Chalcot House. | Westbury. |
| Corsham Court. | Chippenham. |
| The Courts. | Holt. |
| Great Chalfield Manor. | Melksham. |
| Lacock Abbey. | Nr. Chippenham. |
| Littlecote. | Nr. Hungerford. |
| Longleat House. | Warminster. |
| Luckington Court. | Luckington. |
| Lydiard Mansion. | Purton. |
| Malmesbury House. | Salisbury. |
| Mompesson House. | Salisbury. |
| Newhouse. | Redlynch. |
| Philipps House. | Dinton. |
| Pythouse. | Tisbury. |
| Sheldon Manor. | Chippenham. |
| Stourhead. | Stourton, Nr. Mere. |
| Wardour Castle. | Tisbury. |
| Westwood Manor. | Bradford-on-Avon. |
| Wilton House. | Salisbury. |

## WORCESTERSHIRE.
(See Hereford & Worcester)

## NORTHERN IRELAND.

| | |
|---|---|
| Ardress House. | Co. Armagh. |
| Arthur House. | Co. Antrim. |
| Castle Coole. | Co. Fermanagh. |
| Castle Ward. | Co. Down. |
| Derrymore House. | Co. Armagh. |
| Florence Court. | Co. Fermanagh. |
| Mount Stewart. | Co. Down. |
| Mussenden Temple, Bishops Gate & Black Glen. | Castlerock. |
| Printing Press. | Strabane, Co. Tyrone. |
| Rowallane Garden. | Saintfield. |
| Springhill. | Nr. Moneymore, Co. Derry. |
| Templetown Mausoleum. | Co. Antrim. |
| Wellbrook Beetling Mill. | Cookstown, Co. Tyrone. |
| Wilson House. | Co. Tyrone. |

## IRELAND.

| | |
|---|---|
| Adare Manor. | Co. Limerick. |
| Bantry House. | Bantry, Co. Cork. |
| Birr Castle Demesne. | Birr. Offaly. |
| Bunratty Castle. | Nr. Shannon. |
| Castletown House. | Celbridge. |
| Clonalis House. | Castlerea, Co. Roscommon. |
| Johnstown Castle. | Wexford. |
| Knappogue Castle. | Co. Clare. |
| Longfield House. | Nr. Cashel. |
| Mount Usher. | Ashford, Co. Wicklow. |
| National Botanic Gardens. | Glasnevin, Dublin 9. |
| Powerscourt Estate & Gardens. | Co. Wicklow. |
| Riverstown House. | Glanmire, Co. Cork. |

## CLWYD. (WALES)

| | |
|---|---|
| Bodrhyddan Hall. | Nr. Rhyl. |
| Chirk Castle. | Nr. Wrexham. |
| Erddig. | Nr. Wrexham. |

## DYFED. (WALES)

| | |
|---|---|
| Cymerau. | Glandyfl. |
| The Hall. | Angle. |
| Manorbier Castle. | Pembrokeshire. |
| Picton Castle. | Haverfordwest. |
| Tudor Merchant's House. | Tenby. |

## GWENT. (WALES)

| | |
|---|---|
| Chepstow Castle. | Chepstow. |
| Llanfair Court. | Abergavenny. |
| Penhow Castle. | Nr. Newport. |
| Tredegar House. | Newport. |

## GWYNEDD. (WALES)

| | |
|---|---|
| Bodnant Garden. | Tal-y-Cafn. |
| Bodysgallen Hall. | Llandudno. |
| Bryn Bras Castle. | Llanrug. |
| Caernarfon Castle. | Caernarfon. |
| Conway Castle. | Conwy. |
| Gilfach. | Rowwen, Conwy Valley. |
| Gwydir Castle. | Nr. Llanrwst. |
| Harlech Castle. | Harlech. |
| Penrhyn Castle. | Bangor. |
| Plas Mawr. | Conwy. |
| Plas Newydd. | Isle of Anglesey. |
| Portmeirion. | Gwylt Gardens. |
| Ty Mawr. | Gybernant. |

## POWYS. (WALES)

| | |
|---|---|
| Powis Castle. | Welshpool. |
| Tretower Court & Castle. | Crickhowell. |

## SOUTH GLAMORGAN. (WALES)

| | |
|---|---|
| Cardiff Castle. | Cardiff. |
| Castell Coch. | Whitchurch. |
| St. Fagans Castle. | Cardiff. |

## BORDERS REGION. (SCOTLAND)

| | |
|---|---|
| Abbotsford House. | Melrose. |
| Bowhill. | Nr. Selkirk. |
| Dawyck House Gardens. | Stobo. |
| Floors Castle. | Kelso. |
| Kailzie Gardens. | by Peebles. |
| Mellerstain. | Gordon. |
| Traquair House. | Innerleithen. |

## CENTRAL REGION. (SCOTLAND)

| | |
|---|---|
| The House of the Binns. | by Linlithgow. |
| Doune Castle. | Doune. |
| Doune Park Gardens. | Doune. |
| Linlithgow Palace. | Linlithgow. |

| Mestrie Castle. | Menstrie. |
| Stirling Castle. | Stirling. |

## DUMFRIES & GALLOWAY
## REGION. (SCOTLAND)

| Arbigland Gardens. | Kirkbean. |
| Carlyle's Birthplace. | Ecclefechan. |
| Drumlanrig Castle. | Nr. Thornhill. |
| Kinmount Gardens. | Kinmount, Annan. |
| Maxwelton House. | Nr. Moniaive. |
| Rammerscales. | Lockerbie. |
| Threave Gardens. | Dumfries & Galloway. |

## FIFE REGION. (SCOTLAND)

| Culross Palace. | Fife. |
| Falkland Palace. | Fife. |
| Hill of Tarvit. | Fife. |
| Kellie Castle. | Fife. |
| The Town House. | Culross, Fife. |

## GRAMPIAN REGION.
(SCOTLAND)

| Balmoral Castle. | Nr. Ballater. |
| Braemar Castle. | Braemar. |
| Castle of Drum. | Nr. Aberdeen. |
| Castle Fraser. | Sauchen. |
| Craigievar Castle. | Lumphanan. |
| Crathes Castle. | Banchory. |
| Druminnor Castle. | Rhynie. |
| Dinnottar Castle. | Nr. Stonehaven. |
| Haddo House. | Nr. Methlick. |
| Kildrummy Castle Garden. | Donside. |
| Leith Hall. | Kennethmont. |
| Muchalls Castle. | Stonehaven. |
| Pitmedden. | Udny. |
| Provost Ross's House. | Aberdeen. |
| Provost Skene's House. | Aberdeen. |

## HIGHLAND REGION.
(SCOTLAND)

| Cawdor Castle. | Nairn. |
| Dunrobin Castle. | Golspie. |
| Dunvegan Castle. | Isle of Skye. |
| Eilean Donan Castle. | Wester Ross. |
| Hugh Miller's Cottage. | Cromarty. |
| Inverewe. | Poolewe, Wester Ross. |

155

## LOTHIAN REGION.
(SCOTLAND)

| | |
|---|---|
| The Georgian House. | No. 7 Charlotte Square, Edinburgh. |
| Dalkeith Park. | Nr. Edinburgh. |
| Dirleton Castle & Garden. | Dirleton. |
| Edinburgh Castle. | Castlehill, Edinburgh. |
| Gladstone's Land. | Edinburgh. |
| Hamilton House. | Prestonpans. |
| Hopetoun House. | South Queensferry. |
| Inveresk Lodge. | Inveresk. |
| Lamb's House. | Leith. |
| Lauriston Castle. | Edinburgh. |
| Luffness Castle. | Aberlady. |
| Malleny Garden. | Balerno. |
| Palace of Holyroodhouse. | Canongate, Edinburgh. |
| Preston Mill. | Lothian Region. |
| Royal Botanic Garden. | Edinburgh. |
| Winton House. | Pencaitland. |

## STRATHCLYDE REGION.
(SCOTLAND)

| | |
|---|---|
| Achamore. | Isle of Gigha. |
| Bachelors' Club. | Tarbolton. |
| Bellahouston Park. | Paisley Road West. |
| Benmore (Younger Botanic Garden) | Nr. Dunoon. |
| Botanic Gardens. | Glasgow. |
| Brodick Castle. | Isle of Arran. |
| Burns Cottage. | Alloway. |
| Cameron House. | Alexandria. |
| Culzean Castle. | Maybole. |
| Glenapp Castle Gardens. | Ballantrae. |
| Greenbank. | Glasgow. |
| Hunterston Castle & Gardens. | Hunterston, West Kilbride. |
| Inveraray Castle. | Inveraray. |
| Linn Park. | Glasgow. |
| Loch Lomond Park. | Balloch, Dumbartonshire. |
| Pollok House & Park. | Glasgow. |
| Provan Hall. | Glasgow. |
| Provand's Lordship. | Glasgow. |
| Rossdhu. | Luss. |
| Ross Hall Park. | Crookston. |
| Rouken Glen Park. | Glasgow. |
| Souter Johnnie's Cottage. | Kirkoswald. |
| Victoria Park. | Glasgow. |
| Weaver's Cottage. | Kilbarchan. |

## TAYSIDE REGION.
### (SCOTLAND)

| | |
|---|---|
| Angus Folk Museum. | Glamis. |
| Barrie's Birthplace. | Kirriemuir. |
| Blair Castle. | Blair Atholl. |
| Branklyn Garden. | Perth. |
| Drummond Castle Gardens. | Nr. Crieff. |
| Edzell Castle & Gardens. | Edzell. |
| Glamis Castle. | Glamis. |
| Kellie Castle. | Arbroath. |
| Scone Palace. | Perth. |

# ACKNOWLEDGEMENTS

In preparing this book I have received an enormous amount of help from numerous individuals and several organisations, notably the National Trust, the Historic Houses Association and the Department of the Environment. While they have done all they can to help me, I alone must take responsibility for any historical howlers that happen to have crept into the text.

For their special help I would particularly like to thank Lord Ailesbury, Viscountess Bledisloe, Dora Boulton, Patrick C. Burges-Lumsden, Gerald Charrington, Charles Clive-Ponsonby-Fane, H. J. Cole, P. F. D. Duffie, Lord Eliot, Jeremy Elwes, Helen Fairbank, Alan Giles, Alison Heath, P. A. Howe, N. Lambert, Charles Legh, Lord Mansfield, the Duke of Marlborough, Richard V. Myatt, Peter Neate, Pamela Pleydell-Bouverie, Lord Pembroke, Ethne Rudd, Tony Salmon, Rosemary Seymour, Lord Somerleyton, Patrick Telfer Smollett, Sir Hereward Wake, Michael Watson, M. J. M. Westwood and Susan Woodward.

My principal debt of gratitude is to John Hodgson, the Curator of Sudbury Hall in Derbyshire and the Director of Heritage Education Year, who has contributed an enormous amount of material, much sage counsel and his own unique brand of infectious enthusiasm.

GB